The Basque Table

PASSIONATE HOME COOKING

FROM SPAIN'S MOST

CELEBRATED CUISINE

Teresa Barrenechea *with* Mary Goodbody

THE HARVARD COMMON PRESS ❧ BOSTON, MASSACHUSETTS

Bay of

IZARO

Bermeo
Mundaka

Elantxobe

Santurtzi

Guernica
Gernika-Lumo

Ondarroa

Bilbao
Bilbo

Markina-Xemein

CANTABRIA

Vizcaya

CANTABRIAN
MOUNTAINS

Alava

Vitoria
Gasteiz

CASTILLA-LEÓN

CONDADO DE
TREVIÑO

EBRO RIVER

NORTH

Laguardia

30 MILES

50 KILOMETERS

LA RIOJA

SIERRA DE LA
DEMANDA

MAP BY CHARLES BAHNE 1998

❧

Ama, tu me has enseñado todo lo que sabes.
He escrito este libro para tí con mucho cariño.

❧

THE HARVARD COMMON PRESS
535 Albany Street
Boston, Massachusetts 02118

Printed in the United States of America
Printed on acid-free paper

The Library of Congress has cataloged the hardcover edition as follows:
Barrenechea, Teresa
        The Basque table : passionate home cooking from
    one of Europe's great regional cuisines / Teresa
    Barrenechea, with Mary Goodbody.
        p.   cm.
    Includes index.
        ISBN 1-55832-140-3 (hardcover : alk. paper).
        1. Cookery, Basque. 2. Food habits—Spain—País Vasco.
    I. Goodbody, Mary. II. Title.
    TX723.5.S7B37   1998
    641.5946'6—dc21   98-29295

    ISBN-13: 978-1-55832-327-8
    ISBN-10: 1-55832-327-9

Special bulk-order discounts are available on this and other Harvard Common Press books.
Companies and organizations may purchase books for premiums or resale, or may arrange for a
custom edition, by contacting the Marketing Director at the address above.

Cover design by Night & Day Design
Cover photograph by Rita Maas
Maps by Charles Bahne
Text illustrations by Joanna Roy
Interior design by Barbara M. Bachman

2   4   6   8   10   9   7   5   3   1

Contents

❖ MAIN COURSES 98 ❖

❖ BASQUE BASICS 182 ❖

❖ DESSERTS 204 ❖

Acknowledgments

❧

All my friends, you have given me such support and energy. If I leave out anyone here who has helped me in writing this book, I hope you will forgive me.

My deepest gratitude to—

Elise Goodman, my literary agent. Her faith in me and this book was so strong that she would not rest until I sat down to write it. Thank you, Elise. I owe this book to you.

Mary Goodbody, whose help was so important.

The team at the Harvard Common Press, my publisher. Thank you, Bruce Shaw, Dan Rosenberg, Linda Ziedrich, Christine Alaimo, Holly Joe, Laura Christman, Emily Dello Russo, and Alexander Dwinell.

Felix Barrenechea, my father. He keeps me informed on every current trend in my country when I am here in the United States. His enthusiasm is contagious.

José Luis Iturrieta, my dear Basque friend. He "owns" the Basque Country—nobody else loves it as much and knows about it as he does.

Gerry Dawes, my beloved friend with an American body and Spanish heart. I am thankful that he shares his incredible knowledge with me.

My "other family" at my two restaurants, especially Micky Camarillo and Alfredo Mejía, chefs at Marichu Manhattan and Marichu Bronxville, respectively. As their executive chef and teacher, I get all the credit, but they put their hearts on the "burner" every day. Chicho, Joaquín, and Alfredito, thanks to you, too—you all make it possible.

Fina Cortes, my guardian angel at home. She relieves me of domestic tasks and takes such good care of my children.

Lastly, I offer special gratitude and love to Raynold, my husband, and María, Teresa, Alejandro, and Lucas, my children. You have been so patient and generous with me. Thank you.

Food and Wine of the Basque Country

❖

Come and join me on a culinary expedition to my Basque Country. If you have been there already, you know the journey is worthwhile. If you haven't, I can assure you that you will love it.

Among the cities and towns you'll visit in the Basque Country is Bilbao, where I grew up. Bilbao not only made headlines when the new Guggenheim Museum recently opened its doors, but this city is also the largest in the Basque Country. Bilbao is a special place, enveloped in a picturesque landscape of bright green rolling hills and, only minutes away, a deep blue sea. And then there is the food, which makes Bilbao a paradise for gourmets and gourmands alike. Raised with a tremendous passion for cooking, we Basques are blessed with wonderful fish and shellfish from the Gulf of Biscay as well as with extraordinary meats and vegetables. We are proud of our food; we believe that it is the best in the world. After traveling all over Spain and abroad and falling in love with other cuisines, I have come to the conclusion that Basque cooking justly deserves its reputation as being among the best.

It is for this, and because I have cooked all my life, that I want to share my culinary knowledge with you. I hope that this book will fill a void on the cookbook shelves in many homes. It reflects the reality of Basque cooking, both present and past. I concentrate on traditional dishes, deliberately leaving out fashionable Basque *nueva cocina* (nouvelle cuisine) recipes. They would be the subject of a different book.

The 130 recipes included here are authentic, taken from daily life in the Basque Country and recognizable by old and young Basques alike. These dishes are easy to make even for an inexperienced cook. Most of the ingredients are readily available and, when they're not, I usually suggest a substitution. For the most part, too, the recipes are uncomplicated; they could be included in the daily menus of any household. Together, they provide a heart-warming, healthful, and inexpensive diet.

When I arrived in New York in 1989, I was surprised to find no restaurants dedicated to Basque food. I wandered the streets of Manhattan, where you can sample cooking from nearly every remote corner of the globe, but uncovered no Basque food. In 1991, therefore, my husband and I opened our first Marichu restaurant in Bronxville, New York, and in 1994 we opened the second in Manhattan, near the United Nations building. At both restaurants we served traditional Basque cuisine, which included those dishes I grew up with and learned to cook from my mother, Marichu, after whom our restaurants were named.

Both restaurants became popular and well known for authentic Basque and traditional Spanish cuisine. However, unable to keep up with the increasing demands of running two restaurants, we sold our Bronxville location in 1998, concentrating on the one in Manhattan. In 2004, my husband and I decided to return to Spain, where I had been asked to serve as director of sales for an international kitchen appliance manufacturer in Spain. This led us to sell the Manhattan Marichu in late 2004.

So join me on this culinary journey, in which we will make several stops: We will have *pinchos*, the Basque version of tapas; we will explore wonderful Basque sauces, simple but exquisite fish and meat preparations, and also more sophisticated dishes for special occasions. Vegetable dishes and desserts, uncomplicated and delicious, also deserve a close look. Are you ready?

I do not know of any other place in the world where cooking is as revered an art, and as dominant in the national consciousness, as it is in the Spanish Basque Country. Not even across the border, on the French side, can this collective culinary fanaticism be found. It is one of the most important and distinctive traits of our culture. For Basques, food is a major topic of conversation—with the taxi driver, with fellow bus passengers, with friends lying on the beach. Listen to a conversation between Basques, and most likely you will hear what they had for dinner the previous night, what they will have for lunch that same day, or where you can get this or the other unusual ingredient. We Basques happily live for our next meal!

When I was a university student in Bilbao, I did as everybody else did: I met with friends before lunch at a bar for a small glass of wine and a few pinchos. I recall talking about our professors, exams, new books, and so on, but we certainly also talked about new recipes and restaurants. After these daily meetings we went home—to our parents' homes, that is—for lunch (it was and still is unusual for young Basques to leave their parents' homes before marrying or getting a job in a different town or country). Today going home for lunch seems a great luxury to me, but the custom is one of the reasons so many Basques still cook daily with the passion and the recipes of our parents and grandparents. We have not broken the gastronomic tradition.

In the United States, most people consider lunch a light, secondary meal. Not so in the Basque Country, where lunch, like dinner, consists of three courses. This does not mean that lunch is heavy or very filling, but each course is thoughtfully prepared and complements the others, just as at dinner. Basque restaurants, in fact, use the same menu for both lunch and dinner; neither portion sizes nor prices change.

Basque cuisine is revered all over Spain, in the rest of Europe, and all over Latin America as well. It is famous for its simple, straightforward dishes, which make optimal use of the excellent raw materials nature provides. These dishes are part of a cuisine with its own personality, developed over many generations.

Our coastline along the Bay of Biscay helps define Basque cooking. Fish and seafood are all-important, and freshness is key. Fish is usually grilled, sautéed, or lightly fried, and served with one of our classic sauces, such as Biscayne sauce (*salsa vizcaína*), green sauce (*salsa verde*), or black ink sauce (*salsa de chipirón*). Other traditional dishes include robust seafood stews and soups, versions of those originally made by fishermen when out at sea. Anchovies, sardines, and squid are as integral to the Basque diet as are tuna, *bonito*, hake, codfish, shrimp, and turbot. But above all we love salt cod (*bacalao*), which prepared as the Basques do is a delight.

Inland farmers supply us with beef, lamb, pork, and chicken, the wild terrain of the mountains with game of all kinds. True to Basque tastes, we gener-

A Little Background
on the Basque Country

❧ *No one knows* for sure where the Basques came from, but they have lived in what is now north-central Spain and southwestern France as long as history has been been recorded, and far longer. Their language, Euskera, is not even vaguely similar to Castilian, Catalan, or Portuguese, since it is not a Romance language. Some linguists find similarities between Euskera and other pre–Indo-European languages, such as Hungarian and Georgian, but the link is not clear.

The Basque terms Euskadi and Euskal Herria might both be translated as "Basque Country," but their connotations differ. Euskadi refers to the politically established autonomous community formed of three Spanish provinces: Vizcaya, Guipúzcoa, and Alava. Euskal Herria refers to the broader, historically and culturally Basque territory that includes Euskadi, Navarra, and, in France, Labourd, Bassse Navarre, and Soule. In this book I concentrate on the Spanish Basques, and mainly on the inhabitants of Euskadi, although I make short forays into Navarra and also Rioja.

Euskadi, or País Vasco—the Basque Country in the narrow sense—is a triangular region in north-central Spain, with its coastline along the Bay of Biscay in the Atlantic Ocean. The Pyrenees mountains mark the frontier with France. To the east is Navarra, to the south Rioja and Castilla-León, and to the west Cantabria. This location makes the Basque country the link between the Iberian Peninsula and the rest of Europe.

Throughout history, the Basques have enjoyed at least partial local sovereignty. The Romans, Visigoths, and Moslems, who conquered the rest of the Iberian Peninsula, were undoubtedly intimidated by the mountains and passes of the Basque region. The valleys were owned by Basque feudal lords, the *jauntxos*, who determined land ownership, tax collection, the use of the forests, and other matters. After the kingdom of

Castille annexed a great part of the Basque region in the thirteenth century, each king swore to preserve Basque regional law, or *fueros*, under a great oak tree in Guernica that is the symbol of Basque nationality. The *fueros* were upheld until the nineteenth century.

After Franco's death, Spain became a democracy, and in 1979 the nation underwent decentralization. Today the Basque Country is one of Spain's 17 autonomous communities, each of which has its own parliament and government. Thanks to the efforts of the Basque government, even urban Basque children now study Euskera, a language that was banned by Franco.

Of the three provinces that make up the Basque Country, the closest to France is Guipúzcoa; its capital is the beautiful seaside city of San Sebastián (Donostia, in Euskera). Next comes Alava, whose capital is the inland city of Vitoria (Gasteiz, in Euskera), the seat of government for the Basque Country. Vizcaya is the third province; its capital, Bilbao, is the largest and most important city in the Basque Country.

ally serve meats simply roasted or grilled with straightforward sauces, or we cook them in hearty stews.

We insist that our vegetables and fruits be fresh. More often than not, vegetables are part of a salad or other first course. Typical products of our market gardens are red and white shell beans, flat green beans, leeks, tomatoes, potatoes, onions, garlic, and peppers. Other common ingredients are wild mushrooms, apples (especially the delicious Reinetas), fresh berries, and other fruits. My exception to the "fresh only" rule are white asparagus and piquillo peppers from Navarra. Nothing surpasses these canned products for tenderness and subtle flavor.

Our food is delicately seasoned with fresh herbs, mild and hot peppers, a good amount of garlic and parsley, and every now and then a friendly dose of sherry or wine. We use almost no oil besides high-quality, fruity Spanish olive oil, and we use butter only rarely, for baking and for desserts. Desserts are deliciously modest and homey. Our cheeses, made in the *caserios*, our farm-houses, also deserve a special mention. Idiazabal cheese is the most significant one.

We drink wine with most of our meals. The wines produced in the Basque area of Rioja, Rioja Alavesa, can compete with the best in the world, despite the relatively small extent of the vineyards. *Txakoli*, a slightly effervescent white wine, is produced in all three provinces of the Basque autonomous community. On pages 139 to 142 you'll learn more about these and other wines.

This book is organized according to Basque dining custom: There are pinchos for snacks, then first courses, main courses, and desserts for midday and evening meals. As you will see, however, many of the dishes we Basques consider first courses might be served instead as side dishes. This is a matter of taste and custom; we prefer not to mix our dishes, but rather to enjoy them in sequence. Some first courses, such as our hearty soups and stews, would also work well as main dishes, particularly for American lunches and light dinners.

We Basques are proud of our culinary achievements. Our passion for food, having lasted many generations, is still very much alive today. I hope you will come to share in this passion as you follow the recipes on these pages and learn about the food of my beloved homeland.

PINCHOS

Pinchos—or pintxos, *as the Basques spell the word*—are the Basque Country's singular form of the better known Spanish *tapas*. The term derives from the Spanish word *pinchar*, *"to prick,"* because originally *pinchos were always served skewered on wooden toothpicks. Today they may be served either on toothpicks or in small earthenware bowls or on platters; they are eaten as finger food. In concept pinchos are similar to tapas; both are bites of tasty nourishment shared with friends in bars and taverns. But tapas evolved in southern Spain, from the old-time practice*

of laying a slice of bread or meat across the top of a sherry glass (their name derives from the word tapar, *"to cover"). Today tapas must usually be eaten with a fork or spoon, and whereas tapas may be small servings of any dish, pinchos are a distinct set of little dishes that are never served at meals.*

Of course, the social interaction surrounding pinchos is as important as the food. We Basques greatly enjoy meeting friends before lunch or dinner for a small glass of wine and a few pinchos. It is a time when we can discuss the latest soccer game, a new love affair, or, of course, a recipe. And when a delicious little morsel accompanies our conversation, so much the better!

The pinchos I present here are traditional ones, authentic combinations of foods such as hard-cooked eggs, shrimp, anchovies, olives, ham, asparagus, and mushrooms. No matter how simple the preparation, we use fresh, delicious ingredients when we assemble pinchos. And it is not only barkeeps who assemble them. Many home cooks serve pinchos at parties and casual gatherings. They are easy to make and look pretty and inviting on a tray. The innovative chefs working in nueva cocina *restaurants in the Basque Country may be taking pinchos to new heights with exotic combinations of foods and spectacular presentations, but I think the simple ones collected here are excellent samples of these tiny treasures.*

Potato Omelet

Makes 20 pinchos

There is not a bar or a party in Basque Country that does not offer *tortilla de patata* as a pincho. This extremely popular dish is excellent accompanied by a small glass of wine, but it can also be cut into large pieces and served as a light entrée with a green salad, making a fine light meal for vegetarians, especially. *Tortilla de patata* is also common picnic fare, and it's a popular sandwich, or *bocadillo*, filling. I make this omelet often, and it has saved me more than once when I had to make an unplanned meal, because the ingredients are household staples.

The omelet may sound complicated to make, since it is removed from the pan and then returned for further cooking, but after you have tried this once or twice, you will find it is very easy—as long as you have a plate that is a little larger in diameter than the pan.

1 cup olive oil
½ medium onion, chopped
3 medium potatoes, cut into teaspoon-sized pieces (about 1 pound)
Salt
4 large eggs

1. In a large skillet (about 10 inches in diameter), heat the olive oil over medium-high heat. Add the onion, and sauté it for about 5 minutes, until it is light golden. Add the potatoes, and season them to taste with salt. Reduce the heat to medium, and cook the potatoes for about 15 minutes longer, stirring, until they are tender.

2. Raise the heat to medium-high, and cook the potatoes for 1 to 2 minutes longer, until they are lightly browned, crisp on the outside, and soft on the inside. Using a large slotted spoon, remove the potatoes and onion from the pan, and drain them in a colander or on paper towels. Let the oil in the pan cool slightly, then pour all but about 1½ teaspoons into another container to use later.

3. In a large bowl, beat the eggs lightly. Add the potatoes and onion, and mix well. Set the mixture aside for a few minutes.

4. Heat the skillet over high heat, tipping the pan to assure that the oil is evenly distributed. When it is very hot, pour the egg mixture into the pan. Use a spatula to spread the mixture evenly in the skillet. Shake the pan gently to prevent sticking and burning, and cook the omelet for about 1 minute. Reduce the heat to medium, and continue cooking the omelet for 2 or 3 minutes longer, until the eggs begin to set around the edges.

5. Lay over the skillet a plate that is slightly larger in diameter than the skillet. Using one hand to hold the plate in place, invert the omelet onto it. (Do this over a clean work surface for insurance.)

6. Return the empty skillet to the stove, add another 1½ teaspoons of the reserved oil, and heat it over high heat. When the oil is hot, slide the omelet off the plate and into the pan (the uncooked side should be facing down). Shake the pan gently to prevent sticking, and cook the omelet for 1 minute. Reduce the heat to medium, and cook for about 3 minutes longer, until the omelet is set. Slide the omelet onto a serving plate, and let the omelet cool.

7. Cut the omelet into 20 small squares or wedges, and serve them skewered with toothpicks or on top of thin slices of bread.

Croquettes

Makes 15 pinchos

Nobody likes croquettes more than Basques do. We often eat these tasty little morsels before lunch or dinner with a glass of wine, and sometimes we serve them at a cocktail party or as a light meal; children, especially, like them for supper. I have made this master recipe with salt cod, because it is so popular in the Basque Country, but you can substitute the same amount of chopped ham, chicken or turkey, beef, or chorizo sausage meat for the salt cod (making croquettes is a terrific way to use scraps and leftovers from other dishes). Sometimes we make a variety of croquettes and form them into slightly different shapes so that our guests know that one is different from the others.

3 ounces skinned and boned salt cod
1¼ cups olive oil
4 tablespoons unbleached all-purpose flour
1½ cups milk
Salt
2 large eggs, lightly beaten
2 tablespoons dry bread crumbs

1. In a shallow bowl, cover the fish with cold water. Refrigerate the fish for 24 to 36 hours, changing the water every 8 hours or so. Drain the fish on paper towels, and finely shred it with your fingers.

2. In a skillet, heat ¼ cup of the oil over medium heat. Add the salt cod, and sauté it for about 3 minutes. Add 2 tablespoons of the flour, mix well, and sauté for about 2 minutes, until the flour is blended with the cod.

3. In a small saucepan, warm the milk; this makes it easier to blend with the other ingredients. Add 1 cup of the milk to the skillet (keep the remaining ½ cup of milk warm), and mix well to blend the milk with the flour and cod. Bring the mixture to a boil over medium-high heat. Reduce the heat to

medium-low, and cook the mixture, stirring, for about 10 minutes, until it is well blended and hot.

4. Add the remaining $1/2$ cup of milk to the pan, and cook the mixture for about 10 minutes longer, stirring constantly, until it is quite tender. Season it to taste with salt, if needed.

5. Transfer the contents of the pan to a shallow 8-inch-square dish or an oval dish of about the same volume. Spread the mixture evenly. Refrigerate the dish for several hours or overnight, until the mixture is chilled and firm but malleable.

6. Spread the remaining 2 tablespoons of flour on a plate. Put the beaten egg in a shallow bowl. Spread the bread crumbs on a separate plate.

7. With slightly dampened hands, form the cod mixture into walnut-sized balls. Roll each one in flour, dip it in the egg, and then roll it in the bread crumbs to coat it all over. Set each finished ball aside on a wax paper–lined tray. Refrigerate the balls to firm them for at least 15 minutes and as long as several hours.

8. When you're ready to cook the balls, heat 1 to 2 inches of olive oil in a deep skillet. Add four or five croquettes to the hot oil, and cook them, turning them often, for about 1 minute, until they are golden brown. Using a slotted spoon, gently lift the croquettes from the pan, and drain them on paper towels. Continue frying the rest of the croquettes, letting the oil regain its heat between batches. Serve immediately, while they're still hot.

NOTE: *If the croquettes cool off, reheat them in a warm (300°F) oven (not a microwave).*

Eggs Stuffed with Anchovies and Tuna

◆ HUEVO RELLENO DE ANCHOA Y BONITO ◆

Makes 10 pinchos

This very simple recipe, which uses canned tuna and canned anchovy fillets, may seem unusual coming from someone who adores freshly caught fish, but in the Basque Country and neighboring Navarra we are fortunate to have the best canned food in the world. Canning is serious business here, and because the canning companies begin with high-quality fresh ingredients, our canned products are outstanding. If you can locate imported canned fish, use it. Otherwise, use any high-quality canned tuna and anchovies.

5 large hard-cooked eggs
5 tablespoons homemade (page 184) or commercial mayonnaise
One 3-ounce can albacore tuna packed in oil, drained and flaked
5 canned anchovy fillets, chopped

1. Peel the eggs, and slice them in half lengthwise. Carefully remove the yolks, and transfer them to a small bowl.
2. Add the mayonnaise, tuna, and anchovies to the bowl, and mash them with a fork until the mixture is well blended and almost smooth. Spoon the mixture into the egg whites, and serve the eggs chilled or at room temperature.

Egg and Shrimp Pinchos

◆ PINCHO DE HUEVO Y GAMBA ◆

Makes 10 pinchos

Both at midday and in the evening in the Basque Country, most bars serve this pincho.

5 large hard-cooked eggs
10 cooked medium shrimp (see Note and page 16)
3 heaping tablespoons homemade (page 184) or commercial mayonnaise

1. Peel the eggs, and slice them in half lengthwise. Top each egg half with a shrimp and then about 1 teaspoon mayonnaise.
2. Skewer each pincho with a toothpick, and serve immediately.

NOTE: *when I call for medium shrimp, I mean those that are sold in units of 36 ("U36" or "36-count"), which means there are approximately 36 shrimp to the pound.*

❧   *We Basques eat* a lot of shrimp. We buy them as fresh as possible, still in their shells and smelling pleasantly briny. I recommend buying the shrimp on the day you will serve them and cooking them no more than an hour or so before serving.

As soon as you get home with the shrimp, store them in the rear of the refrigerator, where it is coolest. If they will be stored for more than a few hours, set the wrapped package in a small bowl, and place the small bowl in a larger one filled with ice. Refrigerate the shrimp sitting on ice to keep them as cold as possible without freezing.

To cook the shrimp, fill a pot about three-quarters full with water (for a pound of shrimp you will need about 4 cups water). Add 1 teaspoon coarse salt, three black peppercorns, and one bay leaf for every pound of shrimp, and bring the water to a boil over high heat. Add the shrimp, still in their shells. As soon as the water returns to a boil, remove the shrimp with a slotted spoon or mesh skimmer, or drain them in a colander. Without delay, transfer the shrimp to a large bowl filled with ice cubes, ice water, or both, so that the shrimp cool as quickly as possible. Peel the shrimp, which now will be pink, and use them immediately or refrigerate them.

Pinchos Gilda

These pinchos are named after a character in the 1946 eponymous movie starring Rita Hayworth, who played Gilda in the leading role, and Glenn Ford. The Spanish filmgoing public fell in love with the sensual, fiery character played by Hayworth, and so named this enticing and slightly spicy pincho after her.

20 small pitted green olives
10 canned anchovy fillets
10 guindillas, *pepperoncini, or other small hot pickled peppers (see Note)*

On a toothpick, skewer an olive, a folded anchovy, a pepper, and then another olive. Repeat with the remaining ingredients to make 10 pinchos. Serve immediately.

NOTE: *Spanish* guindillas *are very hard to find in this country, but pepperoncini are an excellent substitute.*

Crabmeat Pinchos

* PINCHO DE CANGREJO *

Makes 14 pinchos

In these pinchos, fresh crabmeat crowns thin slices of slender, European-style baguettes, which are crusty on the outside and tender inside. The baguette slices should be about three inches long and one and a half inches wide. Buy the crabmeat from a reputable fishmonger to assure it is as fresh and clean as can be, or shell the crab yourself. Use whatever type of crab is available.

½ pound fresh crabmeat, finely shredded
½ cup homemade (page 184) or commercial mayonnaise
6 scallions, white part only, minced
Fourteen ¼- to ½-inch-thick baguette slices

1. In a small bowl, combine the crabmeat, mayonnaise, and scallions, and mix well.
2. Spread the mixture on the baguette slices, and serve the pinchos at room temperature.

Mushroom Pinchos

◆ PINCHO DE CHAMPIÑÓN ◆

Makes 10 pinchos

Most pinchos can be served either chilled or at room temperature, but these are the exception: Always serve them warm. As they cook, some of the parsley-garlic filling will escape from the mushroom caps, but this should not worry you.

1 tablespoon chopped flat-leaf parsley
2 garlic cloves, minced
30 small mushrooms, 1 to 1½ inches across (about ½ pound), stemmed
¼ cup olive oil
1 tablespoon white wine vinegar
1½ teaspoons paprika
Salt

1. In a small bowl, combine the parsley and garlic. Spoon a little into each mushroom cap.

2. In a skillet, heat the oil over medium heat. Add the mushrooms, filled sides up. Reduce the heat to low, and cook the mushrooms for about 5 minutes, stirring gently to prevent them from sticking but without turning them. Sprinkle them with the vinegar, paprika, and salt, and then turn the mushrooms. Cook them for about 5 minutes longer. Raise the heat to medium, turn the mushrooms again so that the filled sides are facing up, and cook the mushrooms for 2 to 3 minutes longer, until they are fragrant and heated through.

3. Transfer the mushrooms to a plate to cool slightly. When they are cool enough to handle, thread three mushrooms on each toothpick, and serve the pinchos warm.

Spicy Tuna Pinchos

❖ PINCHO DE BONITO PICANTE ❖

Makes 10 pinchos

These quick pinchos are a good example of how convenient it is to have on hand Basque Tomato Sauce (page 186) or your own favorite tomato sauce, homemade or commercial. With the addition of hot pepper flakes, a slightly sweet tomato sauce combines terrifically with the tuna. As for Crabmeat Pinchos (pages 16), the baguette slices should be about 3 inches long.

One 6-ounce can albacore tuna packed in oil, drained and flaked
6 tablespoons Tomato Sauce (page 186)
¹/₂ teaspoon hot red pepper flakes

continued

Ten ¼- to ½-inch-thick slices from a slender,
European-style baguette, lightly toasted

1. In a small bowl, combine the tuna, tomato sauce, and pepper flakes, and mix well.
2. Spread the mixture on the baguette slices, and serve the pincho at room temperature.

Sweet Ham and Lettuce Pinchos

✦ PINCHO DE JAMÓN Y LECHUGA ✦

Makes 10 pinchos

This pincho is a tasty combination of ham and hard-cooked eggs, with lettuce for crunch and fresh flavor. Eat the pincho freshly made, before it gets soggy.

3 large hard-cooked eggs
Ten ¼- to ½-inch-thick slices from a slender, European-style baguette
10 thin slices baked ham, minced
3 leaves green-leaf lettuce, minced
5 tablespoons homemade (page 184) or commercial mayonnaise

1. Cut the eggs into thin lengthwise slices, with each slice containing some yolk (discard the slices that do not have any yolk). You'll need a total of 10 slices. Lay an egg slice on each slice of bread.
2. In a small bowl, combine the ham, lettuce, and mayonnaise, and stir well. Spread an equal amount of the ham mixture on each egg slice, and serve the pincho at room temperature.

Smoked Salmon and Asparagus Pinchos

❖ PINCHO DE ESPÁRRAGO Y SALMON ❖

Makes 10 pinchos

If you have never tried canned white asparagus from Navarra, you are in for a treat. I think it is better than most fresh asparagus, which is saying a lot because I generally prefer fresh vegetables. However, the Navarrans are well known for their superior canned products, and the white asparagus is the shining star in this galaxy. If you can't find Navarra canned white asparagus locally, you can order it from Northern Boulevard (718-779-4971) in Queens, New York.

5 thin slices smoked salmon, each about 8 inches long and 4 inches wide
5 canned white asparagus spears, preferably from Navarra,
or cooked fresh white asparagus
5 tablespoons homemade (page 184) or commercial mayonnaise
Ten 1/4- to 1/2-inch-thick slices from a slender, European-style baguette,
lightly toasted

1. Cut each slice of salmon in half to make 10 pieces, each about 4 inches square.
2. Cut each asparagus spear in half crosswise, then slit each half lengthwise without cutting all the way through.
3. Spread a little mayonnaise on each slice of baguette. (Do not use all the mayonnaise.)
4. Spread the remaining mayonnaise in the slits in the asparagus. Wrap each asparagus spear with a slice of smoked salmon, and place a wrapped spear on each slice of toast. Serve immediately.

Green Pepper, Serrano Ham, and Anchovy Pinchos

❖ Pincho de Pimiento, Jamón y Anchoa ❖

Makes 10 pinchos

The soft-cooked peppers make these pinchos special, and because both the peppers and the eggs can be cooked well ahead of time, the pinchos can be quickly assembled when you are ready to serve them.

3 tablespoons olive oil
1 green bell pepper, seeded and cut into 1-inch-long strips
3 large hard-cooked eggs
Ten ¼- to ½-inch-thick slices from a slender, European-style baguette
10 thin slices serrano ham or prosciutto, each about 3 inches long and
1½ inches wide
10 canned anchovy fillets

1. In a skillet, heat the oil over medium heat. Reduce the heat to medium-low, and add the pepper strips. Sauté them for about 15 minutes, until they are tender. Remove them from the skillet, and let them cool completely.
2. Cut the eggs into thin lengthwise slices, with each slice containing some yolk (discard the slices that do not have any yolk). You'll need a total of 10 slices.
3. Spread a portion of cooled peppers on each slice of bread. Top with a slice of ham, a slice of egg, and an anchovy fillet. Serve at room temperature.

FIRST
COURSES

In the Basque Country, as indeed throughout all of Spain, lunch and

dinner each have three courses—a first course, a main course, and a

dessert. The first course frequently includes greens and other vegetables,

sometimes in the form of a salad, soup, or stew; the main course

consists of meat or seafood usually unaccompanied by a vegetable side

dish. First courses also might include small amounts of meat or seafood,

served with complementary vegetables or alone.

In Basque restaurants serving nueva cocina *(nouvelle cuisine), innovative* chefs have created an endless variety of salads, relying on the wonderful fresh vegetables, farmhouse cheeses, and impeccable seafood available in our region. I have not included these imaginative salads in this book, but instead have assembled a group of more traditional salads that will satisfy the need for fresh greens and that, when made with good ingredients, will rival any nouvelle chef's. My favorite salad, and the one that I think best exemplifies our traditional cuisine, is the Marichu Salad (page 63) which can be composed of nothing more than lettuce, tomatoes, and onions, or can be made more elaborate with the addition of other ingredients, such as hard-boiled eggs, olives, tuna, boiled potatoes, asparagus, or anchovies.

At any time of the day or year in the Basque Country, it's quite common to find a stockpot of soup or a large pot of stew simmering on the back burner of a kitchen stove. This is one tradition that has not changed much since I was a girl. Particularly in the cooler months, we frequently begin our midday or evening meal with a bowl of steaming lentil, leek and potato, or onion soup, or red bean or tuna stew. We make soups and stews using fresh vegetables and fish, chorizo sausages, legumes, and other simple and easily available ingredients; these are not elegant preparations, but they are warm, comforting, and satisfying. Although they are always served as first courses in the Basque Country, you could serve any of the soups and stews in this chapter as the centerpiece of a light meal.

Most important for our first courses, as with all Basque food, is to use the best and freshest ingredients possible. This means fresh-from-the-sea clams and shrimp, precious baby eels, and silvery fresh anchovies; it means tender sweetbreads and bold serrano ham, garden-fresh green beans, and earthy mushrooms. Because these are first courses, quantities can be small, but care and attention is lavished in choosing and preparing the food.

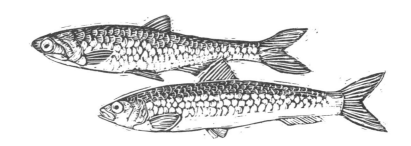

Meats and Seafood

Sweetbreads with Garlic and Parsley

❖ MOLLEJAS AL AJILLO ❖

Serves 6

Rich, delicious sweetbreads are divine as a first course, particularly when pan-fried with parsley and garlic, Basque-style.

1 pound sweetbreads (see Note)
2 carrots, halved
1 leek, halved
Juice of 1 lemon
Salt
2 tablespoons dry bread crumbs
2 tablespoons chopped garlic
2 tablespoons chopped flat-leaf parsley
4 to 5 tablespoons olive oil

1. In a large saucepan or stockpot, combine the sweetbreads, carrots, leek, and lemon juice, and season to taste with salt. Add enough water to cover

continued

the contents by 1 to 2 inches, and bring the water to a boil over medium-high heat. Reduce the heat, and simmer for about 5 minutes. In a colander, drain the sweetbreads and vegetables. When they are cool enough to handle, remove and discard the vegetables.

2. Rinse the sweetbreads with cold water, drain them, and trim away any fat or membrane. Lay the sweetbreads on a kitchen towel, and place a flat plate on top of them. Set a few cans of food or a heavy pan on the plate to weight the sweetbreads, and let them sit in a cool room or in the refrigerator for about 1 hour.

3. Spread the bread crumbs in a shallow dish.

4. Slice the sweetbreads into small pieces, and sprinkle them with salt. Roll the sweetbreads in the bread crumbs, and sprinkle them with garlic and parsley.

5. In a skillet, heat the olive oil over medium-high heat. Add the sweetbreads, and cook them, turning them several times, for 2 to 3 minutes on each side, until they are golden brown and crisp all over. Serve immediately.

NOTE: *Calves' sweetbreads are available in most good butcher shops; lambs' sweetbreads only occasionally are. If you can find lambs' sweetbreads, though, try them for their wonderful flavor. If you're using lambs' sweetbreads, omit step 1, since they do not need as thorough a cleaning.*

Foie Gras with Apples
❧ FOIE-GRAS CON MANZANAS ❧

Serves 4

Foie gras is the fattened liver of waterfowl that are hand-fed for at least 30 days, during which time they are allowed very little exercise. The result is a large liver with a silken texture and glorious flavor. In the United States, it is becoming increasingly easy to buy foie gras. If you can't locate a source, call Hudson Valley Foie Gras (516-773-4400), or visit the website at www.foiegras.com, for the number of a distributor near your home. Owned by my friend Michael Ginor, Hudson

Valley is the largest foie gras producer in the world. Or order foie gras direct from D'Artagnan (800-DARTAGNAN or 973-344-0565), a New Jersey company that ships specialty meats all over the United States.

Although most people associate foie gras with France, we have been enjoying it in the Basque Country for a long time—particularly during the past thirty years, when our cuisine has expanded in scope. The Basque Country, after all, is quite close to Landes, France, a region well known for its geese farms.

There are other ways to prepare foie gras, but I particularly like this simple preparation, in which the liver is quickly sautéed and served over sautéed, lightly sweetened apples. At the very end of cooking, I make a quick pan sauce using port and the fat remaining in the pan; such deglazing is common in Basque cooking, and it's a technique that rarely lets you down.

One duck or goose liver, weighing about 1 pound (see Note)
Salt and fresh-ground white pepper
1 tablespoon unsalted butter
2 firm, tart apples, such as Granny Smith or Fuji, peeled, cored, and
cut into 8 wedges each
1½ teaspoons sugar
3 tablespoons port or other sweet fortified wine

1. Using your fingers, carefully separate the liver into its two sections. For the sake of appearance, try to pull out any visible veins. Cut each liver half crosswise into 1-inch-thick slices. Sprinkle them lightly with salt and white pepper.

2. In a nonstick skillet, heat 1 tablespoon butter over medium heat. Reduce the heat to low, add the apple wedges, and cook them for about 15 minutes, turning them often, until they soften. Sprinkle them with the sugar, raise the heat to medium-high, and shake the pan to prevent burning. Cook the apples for a few minutes longer, until they are golden brown. Arrange four wedges on each of four plates. Cover the plates to keep the apples warm.

3. To cook the liver, heat two nonstick skillets over high heat. When they are

continued

very hot, distribute the liver pieces evenly between the dry skillets (the liver will release all the fat you need), shaking the pans to prevent sticking. Cook the liver for about 2 minutes on each side, until it is golden brown. Remove the pans from the heat to prevent overcooking, and lift the liver from the pans. Drain it on two layers of paper towels.

4. In one of the skillets, combine the fat remaining in both. Add the wine, and turn the heat to high. Cook, stirring, for about 30 seconds, until the sauce is hot and blended.

5. On each plate, arrange a portion of the liver next to the apples, and spoon the sauce over the liver. Serve immediately.

NOTE: *Goose or duck liver is easier to work with chilled rather than at room temperature, when it is too soft to cut cleanly. Chill the liver in the refrigerator for at least an hour.*

Baby Eels in Sizzling Garlic

❖ ANGULAS A LA CAZUELA ❖

Serves 4

Although rare and very expensive, *angulas*, or baby eels, are a heavenly treat. It is traditional to eat sizzling baby eels with a wooden fork, which stays cooler than metal tableware.

½ cup plus 2 tablespoons olive oil
3 garlic cloves, sliced thin
Hot red pepper flakes
1 pound baby eels (see Notes)
Salt

1. In a 10-inch flame-proof earthenware casserole or skillet, heat the oil over medium-high heat. Add the garlic and pepper flakes, and cook for 3 to 4 minutes, until the garlic is golden.
2. Add the eels, sprinkle them with salt, and cook them, stirring, for about 30 seconds, until they are hot and sizzling. Serve immediately.

NOTES: *If you can't get baby eels locally you can order them from Northern Boulevard, a store in Queens, New York, that ships Spanish products all over the United States. Call the store at 718-779-4971.*

Baby eels are sold frozen. Thaw them overnight in the refrigerator. In the morning, gently wipe them dry with a kitchen towel, and then refrigerate them, loosely wrapped, until you are ready to cook them.

Frog Legs in Sizzling Garlic
❖ ANCAS DE RANA AL AJILLO ❖

Serves 4

When my older brothers and I were young, we visited our aunts during the Easter holidays from school. They lived in Markina, a town with access to brooks and small rivers. My brothers, who preferred ocean fishing, nevertheless contented themselves with catching frogs and eels in these waters, and my aunts often prepared the frog legs in this way. I looked forward to this dish whenever we visited. When I serve frog legs today, I encourage my customers to use their fingers to eat them, because they are too tiny to bone easily with a knife and fork.

½ cup plus 2 tablespoons olive oil
10 garlic cloves, minced
1 pound small frog legs (see Note)
Salt
2 tablespoons chopped flat-leaf parsley

continued

1. In a 10-inch flame-proof earthenware casserole or skillet, heat the oil over medium-high heat. Add the garlic, and cook, stirring, for 3 to 4 minutes, until the garlic starts to turn golden.
2. Add the frog legs, sprinkle them with salt, and cook them, stirring gently with a wooden spoon, for about 5 minutes, until they are golden brown and cooked through. Garnish them with parsley, and serve immediately.

NOTE: *Frog legs are sold skinned and frozen in some fish stores, specialty stores, and supermarkets. They may also be purchased fresh in some places, which of course is the best way to buy them. However, frozen frog legs are very good, particularly if they are thawed slowly in the refrigerator. Buy the smallest frog legs you can find; they should be about 3 inches long.*

Sizzling Garlic Shrimp

✦ GAMBAS AL AJILLO ✦

Serves 4

Shrimp is one of my favorite foods, so I nearly always order some cooked this way when I join friends at bars in Bilbao. This lovely appetizer is served throughout Spain.

For this recipe, I use four flame-proof ceramic crocks that are 5 inches in diameter and 1 inch deep. If you are a dexterous cook, prepare all four servings simultaneously; otherwise, cook them one at a time. If you don't have flame-proof crocks this size, you can heat all of the oil and seasonings together in a 12-inch skillet and cook all the shrimp at once.

½ cup olive oil
2 teaspoons chopped garlic
2 teaspoons hot red pepper flakes
2 teaspoons salt
48 medium shrimp, peeled (see Note)
Chopped flat-leaf parsley

1. Divide the oil, garlic, hot pepper flakes, and salt evenly among four earthenware or ceramic flame-proof crocks. Divide the shrimp into four groups of twelve.
2. One at a time or all at once, heat the crocks over high heat for 1 to 1½ minutes, until the oil sizzles. Add the shrimp, and cook them for about 2 minutes, just until they are pink. Immediately remove the crocks from the heat, sprinkle the shrimp with parsley, and serve them still sizzling.

NOTE: *Medium shrimp may be labeled "U36" or "36-count," which means 36 shrimp per pound, or unit.*

Monkfish Béchamel Wrapped in Lettuce with Squid Ink Sauce

❖ ENSALADA DE RAPE TEMPLADO ❖

Serves 2

Because making these little lettuce-wrapped packages is time-consuming, I've written the recipe to serve only two. For a special occasion, though, you might multiply the quantities. This is a *nueva cocina* Basque dish, not a traditional one, but when I tasted it in one of the finest Basque restaurants in Madrid, I fell in love.

continued

6 large green-leaf lettuce leaves

$^1/_4$ cup olive oil

1 tablespoon chopped onion

1 tablespoon unbleached all-purpose flour

$^1/_2$ cup milk (see Notes)

$^1/_3$ cup water (see Notes)

$^1/_4$ pound monkfish, cut into small chunks

Salt

FOR THE SQUID INK SAUCE:

$^1/_4$ cup olive oil

1 medium onion, chopped

1 small garlic clove, minced

1 tablespoon chopped flat-leaf parsley

2 baby squids, cleaned and peeled (see page 177)

1 teaspoon squid ink (see Notes)

Salt

FOR THE GARNISH:

1 tomato, diced

2 scallions, chopped

1 teaspoon drained capers

2 tablespoons extra-virgin olive oil

$1^1/_2$ teaspoons sherry vinegar

Salt

1. To begin preparing the monkfish packages, submerge the lettuce leaves in boiling water for 1 minute. Drain them, and lay them on a plate or tray to dry.

2. In a large skillet or sauté pan, heat the olive oil over medium heat, and sauté the onion for about 5 minutes, until it is golden. Sprinkle it with the flour, and mix well. Pour the milk and water into the pan, stirring gently to prevent lumps, and simmer the mixture for about 10 minutes. Add the

monkfish, season to taste with salt, and cook the fish for about 5 minutes, until it is opaque throughout. Let the fish cool in the pan.

3. Lay the lettuce leaves on a clean, dry work surface, and divide the fish evenly among them. Carefully wrap the leaves around the fish mixture, tucking in the ends to make mounded packages. Set them aside.

4. To prepare the sauce, heat the olive oil in a skillet or sauté pan over medium heat. Add the onion, garlic, and parsley, and sauté for about 5 minutes, or until the onion softens. Put the baby squid in the pan, and cook, stirring gently, for about 5 minutes longer so the squid imparts its flavor to the sauce. Remove the squid from the pan, and reserve it for another use. Stir in the squid ink and salt to taste, and boil the sauce over high heat for about 5 minutes to cook the squid ink.

5. Transfer the sauce to a blender or food mill, and purée it. Or strain the sauce through a fine-mesh strainer.

6. To prepare the garnish, combine the tomato, scallions, capers, olive oil, vinegar, and salt to taste in a small bowl. Stir gently.

7. Arrange three lettuce bundles on each plate in a triangular pattern. Spoon the garnish between them, and drizzle the plate with a little sauce.

NOTES: *You can substitute 1 cup of clam broth for the water and milk. To make clam broth, cook clams in lightly salted water until they open. Drain them, reserving 1 cup of the cooking liquid for this recipe and the clams for another use. Of course, making clam broth is convenient only if you are preparing clams for another dish or meal.*

Squid ink is available in many fish stores and some specialty stores. If you can't find it, you can take it from squids, but you'll need a lot of squids to produce 1 teaspoon ink. You can, however, substitute cuttlefish ink; you'll need only one or two cuttlefish to produce enough.

Try putting the sauce into a plastic squeeze bottle (such as a plastic ketchup bottle), so you can squeeze it out decoratively onto the plate.

❧ *Traditional Basque dishes* such as the ones in this book have been the foundation and source of inspiration for many talented chefs who, knowing the basic rules of Basque cuisine, are entitled to break them to create original, signature dishes. We Basques can proudly say that our avant-garde chefs can compete with the most renowned ones in the world; some *nueva cocina vasca* chefs, for instance, have been granted the top rating by the Michelin Guide. But in their homes, if they are men, their mothers or wives probably do the cooking, since now as in the past most Basque men cook only in restaurants and in *txokos*, their gastronomical societies. At home, these chefs no doubt indulge in many of the dishes I describe here.

Snails in Biscayne Sauce

❧ Caracoles a la Vizcaína ❧

Serves 6

If I had to choose just one dish that reminds me the most of my mother, Marichu, it would have to be this one. When I moved to Madrid as a young woman, I always journeyed home for Christmas. On my way I literally dreamed about these snails, which are traditional holiday fare among the Basques. But, more often than not, the delectable morsels, painstakingly prepared, were nearly gone by the time the dish got to me! This is because in my parents' house the men are served first, and my brothers never held back when it came to the snails—or any other food. This was torture for me! I so loved them.

Although it takes a while to make this dish, I do so in the restaurant over the holidays, using my mother's recipe. One year, an Italian customer came to me with tears in his eyes, saying that snails were his favorite Christmas dish, and that we had prepared them exactly as his family had in Italy.

The snails taste even better if cooked a day ahead of time, refrigerated, and then gently reheated before serving.

2 pounds brown land snails (see Notes)
Coarse salt
1 leek, trimmed, washed, and sliced (see page 68)
1 medium carrot, sliced
2 small onions, 1 left whole, 1 minced very fine
1 bunch flat-leaf parsley
2 bay leaves
¼ cup plus 2 tablespoons olive oil
¼ pound serrano ham or prosciutto, minced very fine
¼ chorizo sausage, minced very fine
2 cups Biscayne Sauce (page 187)
2 hard-cooked egg yolks, chopped
1 teaspoon hot red pepper flakes

1. To clean the snails, put them into a large colander, put the colander on a plate or in a bowl, and sprinkle the snails with two or three generous fistfuls of coarse salt. Rub the salt over the snails with your hands, then refrigerate the snails with the colander and plate for 2 to 8 hours, or leave them at room temperature for 2 to 3 hours. The snails will release a viscous secretion. Rinse them well under cool running water. Repeat the salting and rinsing process two or three times, until the water runs clear when the snails are rinsed. Transfer the snails to a stockpot.

2. Add enough water to the stockpot to cover the snails by 1 to 2 inches. Bring the water to a boil, and cook the snails over medium-high heat for about 30 minutes. (At this point, the snails will smell unpleasant.) Drain the snails and rinse them thoroughly under cool, running water. Return the snails to the stockpot. They now are clean.

3. Add fresh water to the snails to cover them by 2 to 3 inches. Add the leek, carrot, whole onion, parsley, and bay leaves, and season with a teaspoon or so of salt. Bring the contents to a boil over medium-high heat. Reduce the

continued

heat, and simmer vigorously for about 1 hour. Drain the snails, and set them aside. Discard the vegetables and bay leaves.

4. Heat the olive oil in a skillet or sauté pan over low heat, and sauté the minced onion for 6 to 7 minutes, until it is softened. Add the ham and sausage, and sauté for about 5 minutes, until the sausage is lightly browned. Add the Biscayne Sauce, and cook the mixture, stirring, for 1 to 2 minutes until it is heated through and well mixed.

5. Stir in the snails, mixing them well with the sauce. Add the egg yolks and pepper flakes, stir gently, and cook for about 10 minutes, until the flavors blend. Serve by spooning the mixture onto small plates. Use toothpicks to extract the snails from the shells.

NOTES: *Land snails, also called vineyard snails and* petit-gris *snails, are available fresh in some fish markets, specialty markets, and supermarkets, but usually must be special-ordered. Be sure to order them from a reputable market.*

If you can't get fresh snails, you can use cleaned snails still in their shells, the kind sold in cans for French dishes such as escargots à la Bourguignonne *or* escargots à l'Arlesienne. *If you do, skip steps 1 and 2 and begin the recipe with step 3, draining the snails or not before putting them in the stockpot.*

Baked Sardines

❖ SARDINAS ASADAS ❖

Serves 4

Europeans eat fresh sardines far more often than Americans do, but these little fish are becoming more available in U.S. markets, and adventuresome diners are finding them to be delicious—a far cry from canned sardines. This is a very boldly flavored dish, and therefore not for those who do not like an intense fish flavor. Also, some people may object to having to separate the bones from the fish at the table.

24 fresh sardines, cleaned, heads discarded (about 2 pounds; see Note)
Coarse salt
¼ cup olive oil
2 tablespoons minced garlic
2 tablespoons minced flat-leaf parsley
1 tablespoon dry bread crumbs
4 cups mixed baby greens

1. Preheat the oven to 450°F.
2. Lay the sardines on a plate, and sprinkle them with salt.
3. Spread the oil in a baking dish large enough to hold the sardines in a single layer. Arrange the sardines in the dish, and sprinkle them with the garlic, parsley, and bread crumbs. Bake the sardines for about 10 minutes, just until they are cooked through.
4. Spread the greens on a platter, and the sardines around them. Serve.

NOTE: *Sardines are immature pilchards, which are members of the herring family. If necessary, substitute fresh anchovies for the sardines.*

Clams Bilbao-Style

❖ ALMEJAS A LA BILBAÍNA ❖

Serves 4

Manila clams, increasingly available in the United States, are much like the clams I ate when growing up in Bilbao. Small and sweet, they are ideal for this dish.

I have always made this dish in an earthenware casserole, for several reasons: These casseroles hold heat beautifully and promote even cooking; they are attractive enough to bring to the table for serving; and, finally, I was taught to cook using them and so fully appreciate their value. However, you can use another shallow casserole. Be sure it is flame-proof.

continued

3 dozen Manila, littleneck, or cherrystone clams, well scrubbed (see Note)
3 cups water
⅓ cup olive oil
2 garlic cloves, minced
1 tablespoon unbleached all-purpose flour
Salt
2 tablespoons chopped flat-leaf parsley
½ cup dry white wine

1. Put the clams into a large bowl or pot, and cover them with lightly salted cold water. Using your hands, swish the clams through the water, and then let them sit in the water for about 30 minutes. Drain them, and rinse them well.

2. In a large saucepan, combine the clams and the 3 cups water, and bring the water to a boil over medium-high heat. Cook the clams for about 5 minutes, stirring them with a wooden spoon until they open. Drain the clams, reserving the cooking liquid. Discard any clams that have not opened.

3. Pour the olive oil into a shallow flame-proof casserole, and heat it over very low heat to prevent the casserole from cracking. Add the garlic, and cook it, stirring, for about 2 minutes, until it begins to turn golden. Sprinkle the flour over the garlic, and stir with a wooden spoon until the flour is well mixed with the oil and garlic. Add 2 cups of the reserved cooking liquid, the salt, and the parsley, bring the mixture to a boil, stirring occasionally, and cook for about 5 minutes.

4. Add the wine and clams, and gently shake the casserole to distribute the ingredients evenly and to coat the clams with the sauce. Add a tablespoon or so more of the reserved cooking liquid, if necessary, to maintain a sauce-like consistency. Cook for 2 to 3 minutes longer, until the sauce thickens slightly and the dish is heated through. Serve the clams and sauce immediately, spooned into shallow soup bowls.

NOTE: *A reputable fishmonger should be able to supply you with Manila clams, although you may have to call ahead to order them. If they are not available, substitute littleneck or slightly larger cherrystone clams. Cockles are a good substitute, too, although they may be hard to find.*

❧ *Flame-proof clay casseroles* are very common in Spain. I like to use them because they keep cooked food warm and, since they are decorative, they can double as serving dishes. They come in sizes ranging from 5 inches (recommended for individual portions of sizzling garlic shrimp or baby eels) to 12 inches or wider. The depth varies depending on the size; the small ones are 1 inch deep, the bigger ones as deep as 3 inches.

In the United States, flame-proof earthenware casseroles are available in many kitchenware stores and some large specialty-foods stores. If you can't find them locally, you can order them from Northern Boulevard (718-779-4971).

Even if the label says it is flame-proof, a clay casserole must be treated to prevent cracking before it is used over direct heat. Put your new casserole into a large kettle, cover it with cold water, and leave it overnight. The next day, boil the casserole for 30 minutes, making sure that it is always covered by water.

When you first use your earthenware casserole over direct heat, place a flame tamer (an iron disk) under the casserole to keep it from cracking. Later you may find this isn't necessary.

Crayfish in Hot Sauce

✦ CANGREJOS DE RÍO EN SALSA PICANTE ✦

Serves 4

Crayfish, often referred to as crawfish or crawdads, are small, freshwater crustaceans that are especially sweet and succulent. They are greatly enjoyed throughout the Basque Country and France as well as by Cajuns and Creoles. Crayfish resemble tiny lobsters, and like lobsters they turn bright red when cooked. Also as with lobsters, it is best to cook crayfish live just before eating them; they taste freshest and sweetest this way. The cooking method here, however, will not appeal to everyone, so I urge sensitive cooks to read the recipe before deciding whether to make the dish. If you do make it, you will be rewarded with a delicious—if slightly messy—first course.

You will want to pick up the cooked crayfish with your fingers and extract the meat with a small pick or tiny fork.

1 pound live crayfish (see Note)
1 cup white wine
1 cup Tomato Sauce (page 186)
Hot red pepper flakes (optional)

1. Put the crayfish into a large colander, and rinse them under cool running water. Take care that their small claws don't pinch your fingers. Lift a crayfish from the colander, grasping it in the center of its body. At the end of the tail are three flippers. Grab the middle flipper, and, while twisting it, pull on it to remove it and the attached intestine. Discard the flipper and intestine, and put the crayfish into a large skillet. Put the lid on the skillet to keep the crayfish contained. Repeat with the remaining crayfish.

2. Add the wine to the skillet, cover the skillet, and bring the wine to a boil over high heat. Boil the crayfish for 5 minutes, adjusting the heat to prevent boilovers. When the crayfish turn bright red, drain them in a colander, and rinse them under cool running water. Rinse them well, since they will have exuded some grit while boiling. Return the crayfish to the skillet.

3. Add the sauce to the skillet, and heat it over medium-high heat. Season it to taste with hot pepper flakes. Cook for about 10 minutes, until the sauce is hot and the flavors are blended. Serve the crayfish and sauce in shallow bowls.

NOTE: *Depending on where you live, you may have to call ahead to order crayfish from a fishmonger. Choose a reputable one.*

Fisherman's Rice with Clams

❖ ARROZ CON CHIRLAS ❖

Serves 4

When I was a child, our family spent the summers near the beach in Mundaka, a small coastal village. The closest beach was called Laidatxu (the suffix *-txu* is a Basque diminutive; in Spanish the same suffix is *-chu*). Although we loved piling into the boat with my father for the trip across the channel to the larger beach, called Laida, we always had a good time on Laidatxu, too. My younger brothers, Angel and Iñigo, were particularly proud of the clams they dug on this beach, as they tried to emulate the more impressive catches brought home by my older brothers, who ventured farther from home to fish. My mother made this clam dish to honor the little boys, and it became a family favorite.

Because I prefer this dish a little soupy, I add an extra ¹/₂ cup hot water about 5 minutes before the end of cooking. Leave this out if you like your rice drier.

continued

1 dozen Manila, littleneck, or cherrystone clams, well scrubbed (see Notes)
3 cups water
¼ cup plus 2 tablespoons olive oil
1 small garlic clove, minced
1½ cups medium-grain rice
1 tablespoon chopped flat-leaf parsley
Salt
½ cup hot water (optional)

1. Put the clams into a bowl or pot, and cover them with lightly salted cold water. Using your hands, swish the clams through the water, and then let them sit in water for about 30 minutes. Drain them, and rinse them well.

2. In a large saucepan, combine the clams and the 3 cups water, and bring the water to a boil over medium-high heat. Cook the clams for about 5 minutes, stirring them with a wooden spoon until they open. Drain them, reserving the cooking liquid. Discard any clams that have not opened. Add enough water to the reserved cooking liquid to total 3 cups.

3. In a pot, heat the oil over medium-high heat, and cook the garlic for 3 to 4 minutes, stirring, until it is softened. Before the garlic begins to brown, add the rice, and stir to mix it with the garlic and oil.

4. Add the reserved cooking liquid and water, and bring the contents to a boil. Add the clams and parsley, and season to taste with salt. Reduce the heat, cover the pan, and simmer for about 20 minutes or until the rice is cooked and most of the liquid is absorbed. If you like a soupy consistency, add ½ cup hot water to the pot about 5 minutes before the end of cooking. Let the pan stand off the heat, covered, for about 10 minutes so the flavors blend. Serve in shallow bowls.

NOTES: *During the last few minutes of the standing time, you might place the saucepan in a large container of cold water to prevent the rice from sticking to the bottom of the pan. Do not let the pan sit in cold water for very long, though, or the rice will cool.*

You may have to order Manila clams from a reputable fishmonger. If they are not available, substitute littleneck or slightly larger cherrystone clams. Cockles are a good substitute, too, although they may be hard to find.

❧ *Arguably the most exotic* product of the sea, these barnacles may not look appealing, but their flavor is simply sublime. Europeans have been eating *percebes*, or gooseneck barnacles, for centuries; the Latin word for them is *pollicipedes*. In 1652, when the great painter Diego de Velázquez spent time in the Basque Country, he became enamored of the small sea creatures. On a commission from the king of Spain to paint a picture of Infanta Maria Teresa's wedding to Luis XIV, the king of France, Velázquez spent several months in the region, during which he reportedly feasted on the barnacles whenever possible. He raved about them when he returned to Madrid, and epicures have been singing their praises ever since.

The tube-shaped barnacles grow in clusters on rocks in deep waters, which makes them difficult to harvest, since the rocks are often bashed by large, rough waves, even at low tide. For this reason the barnacles are usually reserved for special occasions at home, and served in mainly the finer restaurants in the Basque Country. They are nearly impossible to buy in the United States, although they grow in Alaska, but because they are so much a part of our cuisine, I wanted to write about them. Even if you never cook them, I hope you will try them in a restaurant if you visit the Basque Country.

If you can acquire some gooseneck barnacles, boil them in salted water for only about 3 minutes, and then remove the pot from the heat. Let the barnacles stand, covered, for about 10 minutes. Drain them, and serve them as plain as can be. Gooseneck barnacles are best eaten just by themselves, without sauce or other adornment.

Spider Crabs Donostia-Style

❖ Txangurro Donostiarra ❖

Serves 4

In this recipe you can use any large crabs, such as stone crabs. But if you ever come across a spider crab, buy it. Do not let its name or appearance discourage you; it is the most splendid crab, one we cherish in the Basque Country and pay dearly for. Spider crabs are imported to the United States, but, perhaps because they look like giant spiders, most fishmongers do not market them. This recipe, developed at the turn of the century by Shishito Ibarguren, a legendary chef from San Sebastián (Donostia, in Euskera), is the classic one for spider crabs. If you order spider crabs in a restaurant in the Basque Country, most likely they will be prepared precisely in this way. Ibarguren is known also for opening a cooking school for women, where many of the best domestic cooks of the day trained before going to work for affluent families.

FOR THE CRABS:

Coarse salt

2 leeks, white parts only, minced (see page 68)

1 bunch flat-leaf parsley

1 medium onion, halved

Four 2-pound spider or other large crabs, such as large stone crabs

FOR THE SAUCE:

½ cup olive oil

3 tablespoons butter

2 medium onions, minced

2 medium carrots, minced

1 garlic clove, minced

2 tablespoons Tomato Sauce (page 186)

½ cup brandy or cognac

½ cup sweet Spanish sherry

2 tablespoons chopped flat-leaf parsley
2 or 3 tablespoons fresh bread crumbs
2 or 3 tablespoons unsalted butter, chopped

1. To cook the crabs, combine in a large stockpot enough water to cover the crabs (2 to 3 quarts, depending on the size of the pot) and 2 tablespoons salt for every quart of water. Bring the water to a boil over high heat. Add the leeks, parsley, and onion, and return the water to a boil. Add the crabs, cover the pot tightly, and bring the water to a boil again. Boil the crabs for 12 minutes, until they turn red. Remove the pot from the heat, and let the water cool to lukewarm.

2. To prepare the sauce, heat the oil and butter in a skillet over medium-low heat. When the butter melts, add the onions, carrots, and garlic, and sauté the vegetables for about 15 minutes, until they soften. Stir in the Tomato Sauce.

3. Holding a crab over a bowl, pull off the top shell, and then remove the crabmeat from the body and legs, allowing the liquid to collect in the bowl. Clean the empty top shell under running water, and set it aside to drain. Do the same with the other crabs.

4. Add the crabmeat, accumulated liquid, brandy or cognac, and sherry to the pan. Bring the contents to a simmer over medium heat, and cook them gently for about 10 minutes, until the flavors blend.

5. Preheat the broiler.

6. Spoon the crabmeat mixture into the top shells, and arrange the filled shells on a broiling rack. Sprinkle with parsley, bread crumbs, and bits of butter, and broil until the butter melts and the crumbs brown. Serve hot.

❧   *Sherry is traditionally* made in Andalucía, the large region that runs along Spain's South Atlantic and Mediterranean coasts. Here, the town of Jerez de la Frontera has long been famed for its production of *jerez*—or *sherry*, as the English mispronounced the word—the golden wine named for the town. The best known categories of sherry are *fino* and *manzanilla*, both pale, straw-gold wines, fresh tasting and impeccably dry. Always served chilled, they are the ideal accompaniment for pinchos or tapas. Cream sherries, very popular in northern Europe and North America, are smooth and rich with a warm aftertaste, and as such make excellent dessert wines. These should always be served at room temperature.

Whereas locals are often seen ordering sherry in Andalusian bars and taverns, this is not a particularly common sight in the Basque Country. We Basques appreciate good sherry now and then, but as a rule we prefer red Rioja wines.

We cook with sherry, however, and when we do so, we follow the golden rule of cooking: The better the ingredients, the better will be the finished dish. This means using respectable sherry when a recipe calls for it, rather than relying on cheap "cooking sherry." Because I rarely call for much sherry in a recipe, and because the wine keeps quite well once it is opened, this rule should be easy for you to follow.

Montilla, in the province of Córdoba, is another region that produces very fine wines. Outside of Spain, Montilla is less known than Jerez, but its *finos*, round *amontillados*, full-bodied *olorosos*, and sweet Pedro Ximénez wines deserve a close look. All of these are available in the United States. I am particularly fond of Fino Alvear, from one of the oldest wineries of Spain, founded in 1729. Serve this wine chilled with the pincho or tapa of your preference.

Marinated Fresh Anchovies

❖ ANCHOAS FRESCAS MARINADAS ❖

Serves 4

Marinated fresh anchovies are very commonly served before lunch or dinner in the Basque Country. Fresh anchovies are not nearly as salty or strong tasting as those you buy canned, and they last for days when marinated in the refrigerator. The fish look rather like sardines, although they are never more than 3 inches long; they have a blue-silver coloring that shimmers and shines in the light. When I find fresh anchovies, I always buy twice the amount I need. I pan-fry half and marinate the rest, as described here.

If you can't find fresh anchovies, substitute small fresh sardines.

1 pound fresh anchovies, cleaned and filleted (see Notes)
1 cup white wine vinegar
1/4 teaspoon hydrogen peroxide (optional; see Notes)
Salt
2 garlic cloves, minced
2 tablespoons chopped flat-leaf parsley
1/2 cup plus 2 tablespoons extra-virgin olive oil

1. In a shallow glass or ceramic bowl, arrange the anchovy fillets skin-side down. Add the vinegar and the peroxide, if you're using it. Cover the bowl, and refrigerate it for at least 24 hours.
2. Drain the anchovies. Lay them in single layers in a shallow serving dish or individual dishes, and sprinkle them with salt and the garlic and parsley. Add the olive oil, cover the anchovies, and refrigerate them for up to 7 days.

continued

NOTES: *To clean the anchovies, cut off the heads, and rinse the fish under cool running water. Slit each fish in half, and lift out the central bone. Scrape away any membranes or intestines. Separate the fillets, and drain them on paper towels.*

Hydrogen peroxide—in the dilute form you probably have in your medicine cabinet—is used to whiten the anchovies, which for authenticity should look very pale when marinated. If you prefer, though, you can leave it out.

TXOKOS, MEN'S CLUBS OF TASTE

❧ *Traditionally the exclusive domain of men,* the Basque gastronomic societies, called *txokos*, thrive in every corner of the Basque Country, with 15 to 100 members each. As often as once a week, the men spend the evening cooking, drinking, and eating. Professionals and laborers join together in the kitchen to cook, sit side by side to eat, and equally share the costs involved.

The first such society was reportedly founded in 1870 in San Sebastián. As the concept caught on, other *txokos* quickly sprang up, in every city and nearly every village in the Basque country. No doubt the clubs originated because men, who were forbidden by custom to cook at home, felt the need of a culinary outlet. Today women are sometimes admitted to the *txokos*, but only as guests.

Without question, some of the best food in Spain is prepared at these clubs, but, because they are closed to everyone but their members and members' guests, outsiders rarely have an opportunity to sample the cooking.

Vegetable Stew
❖ P ISTO A LA B ILBAÍNA ❖

Serves 4

Although in Spain this is a first course, you may prefer to serve it as a side dish, or with wedges of fried or toasted white bread as a light supper.

6 tablespoons olive oil
3 or 4 green bell peppers (about 1 pound), diced
1 medium onion, chopped
4 zucchini (about 1 pound), peeled and diced
Salt
1 cup Tomato Sauce (page 186) or 2 to 3 tomatoes (about 1 pound), diced
4 large eggs, lightly beaten

1. In a 10- to 12-inch skillet, heat the olive oil over medium heat. Add the peppers and onion, and sauté them for about 5 minutes, until the onion softens. Add the zucchini, stir, and season to taste with salt. Reduce the heat to low, and cook the stew uncovered for about 30 minutes, stirring occasionally, until the vegetables are very soft.

continued

2. Stir the Tomato Sauce or diced tomatoes into the other vegetables, and cook for 2 to 3 minutes to blend the flavors.

3. Add the eggs, and stir gently to mix them thoroughly with the vegetables. Serve the *pisto* as soon as the eggs are set, while the mixture is still moist.

Marichu-Style Green Beans

◆ VAINAS MARICHU ◆

Serves 4

I like to make this dish in the late spring, when the beans are tender and sweet and the new potatoes, *patatas nuevas*, are at their best.

2 pounds green beans, preferably flat ones
2 large new potatoes (about 1 pound), peeled and cut into small chunks
4 medium carrots, cut into small chunks
5 tablespoons olive oil
2 garlic cloves, sliced

1. Trim the ends from the beans, and halve the beans crosswise. Pull the strings from any that are a little tough or oversized.

2. In a stockpot, bring 2 quarts lightly salted water to a boil over high heat. Add the beans. Cook the beans, uncovered, over medium-high heat for about 15 minutes, until they are tender. Using a slotted spoon, lift the beans from the water and transfer them to a colander to drain.

3. Add the potatoes and carrots to the pot, and return the water to a boil. Cook the potatoes and carrots over medium heat for about 15 minutes, until the potatoes are fork-tender. Drain the vegetables. (You can reserve the cooking liquid, if you like, to make a light soup with small pasta pieces.) Transfer the beans, potatoes, and carrots to a serving dish.

4. In a small saucepan, heat the oil over medium heat. Add the garlic, and cook it for 3 to 4 minutes, until it is golden (do not let it burn). Pour the hot oil and garlic over the vegetables, toss them gently, and serve them immediately.

Potatoes in Green Sauce

✦ PATATAS EN SALSA VERDE ✦

This first course exemplifies much about popular Basque dishes: It calls for commonly available ingredients, it could not be easier to prepare, and it tastes great. The fresh parsley gives the dish its lovely color and adds significantly to its fresh flavor. Garnishing the servings with egg wedges, a common practice in Basque cooking, makes the dish especially pretty.

¼ cup olive oil

½ medium onion, minced

1 garlic clove, minced

4 large potatoes, peeled and sliced ¼ inch thick

6 cups warm water

Salt

1 cup fresh or frozen green peas

¼ cup chopped flat-leaf parsley

1 hard-cooked egg, cut into wedges (optional)

1. In a large saucepan or stockpot, heat the olive oil over medium heat, and add the onion and garlic. Sauté them for about 5 minutes, until the onion begins to brown. Add the potatoes, stir to coat them with the oil, and sauté them for about 5 minutes longer, until they begin to soften.
2. Add the warm water, season with salt, and bring the contents to a boil over medium-high heat. Reduce the heat, and cover the pan. Simmer the potatoes for about 20 minutes, until they are fork-tender. Stir in the peas and parsley, and cook for about 5 minutes more, until the peas are tender and heated through. Ladle the mixture into shallow bowls, and serve it garnished with egg wedges, if you like.

Vegetable Medley

Serves 6

Because making this dish is time-consuming, my mother did not prepare it as frequently as we all wanted when my brothers and sisters and I were growing up in Bilbao. Much later, when I had children of my own, I understood her reluctance. And so, like her, I generally reserve this dish for special occasions, usually in the springtime, when the vegetables are in season. I typically serve this as a first course, but it could be a side dish, too.

6 small globe artichokes, tough outer leaves discarded and stems and tips trimmed

1 lemon, halved

¼ cup all-purpose flour

2 heads green-leaf lettuce, cored and divided into leaves

6 Swiss chard stems, white parts only

½ cup milk

1 small cauliflower head, cut into florets

6 small new potatoes, peeled and cut into chunks

6 medium carrots, cut into chunks

2 cups fresh green peas

3 large eggs, lightly beaten

1 cup olive oil

6 slices serrano ham or prosciutto, minced

1 cup warm homemade (page 195) or canned beef broth

Salt

2 hard-cooked eggs, each cut into 4 wedges

1. Rub the artichokes with a lemon half.

2. In a stockpot, bring 4 to 5 cups of lightly salted water to a boil over high heat. Add 1 tablespoon of the flour and the second lemon half, and stir gently. Add the artichokes, and cook them over medium-high heat (or at a

low boil) for about 30 to 45 minutes, until they are tender. Drain them in a colander, and set them aside. When they are cool enough to handle, cut them in half lengthwise.

3. While the artichokes cook, bring 3 to 4 cups of lightly salted water to a boil over medium-high heat in a large saucepan. Cook the lettuce leaves, fully submerged, for about 5 minutes, until they are wilted. Carefully lift the leaves from the water, and drain them in a colander, pressing them against the side of the colander with the back of a spoon to extract as much moisture as possible.

4. Let the water return to a boil, add the Swiss chard, and cook it for about 15 minutes, until it is fork-tender. Drain it, and set it aside.

5. In the stockpot, bring another 4 to 5 cups of lightly salted water to a boil over high heat. Add the milk and the cauliflower, and cook the cauliflower over medium-high heat (at a low boil) for about 15 minutes, until it is tender. Drain it, and set it aside.

6. While the cauliflower cooks, bring 3 to 4 cups of lightly salted water to a boil over high heat in a separate stockpot. Add the potatoes and carrots, and cook them over medium-high heat (at a low boil) for about 15 minutes, until they are fork-tender. Drain them, and set them aside.

7. In the pan in which you cooked the lettuce and chard, bring 2 to 3 cups of lightly salted water to a boil over high heat. Add the peas, and cook them over medium-high heat (at a low boil) for about 5 minutes. Drain them, and set them aside.

8. Preheat the oven to 350°F.

9. Spread the remaining 3 tablespoons of flour on a flat plate or a wax paper–lined tray. Put the eggs into a shallow bowl. In a large skillet, heat $^3/_4$ cup of the olive oil over medium-high heat.

10. While the oil heats, tear the lettuce into small pieces, and form them into 2-inch patties with your fingers.

11. Dredge the artichokes, lettuce patties, and Swiss chard in the flour, and then dip them in the eggs. When the oil in the skillet is hot, reduce the heat to medium. Cook the artichokes, lettuce, and chard in the skillet, a few pieces at a time so as not to crowd the pan, for 3 to 4 minutes, turn-

continued

ing them once, until they are lightly browned. Lift the vegetables from the skillet, and drain them on paper towels.

12. In a large casserole, arrange all the vegetables attractively in groups so that each type is visible.

13. Heat the remaining ¼ cup oil in the skillet over medium-high heat, and add the ham. Sauté it for 2 to 3 minutes, until it is lightly browned. Pour the ham, oil, and broth over the vegetables, and season them to taste with salt. Arrange the eggs over the top of the vegetables, cover the casserole, and bake for 10 to 15 minutes, until the vegetables are heated through. Serve immediately.

Mushrooms with Scrambled Eggs

❖ REVUELTO DE SETAS ❖

Serves 4

We Basques like to combine scrambled eggs with vegetables, such as the mushrooms here. If you happen to be in the Basque Country in the springtime, try this dish prepared with the mushrooms called *perretxikos*—they make a meal fit for the gods! But shiitakes are very good, too.

6 tablespoons olive oil
¼ medium onion, minced
¼ pound shiitake mushrooms, stemmed and broken into small pieces (see Note)
Salt
6 large eggs, lightly beaten
2 tablespoons chopped flat-leaf parsley

1. In a skillet about 10 inches wide, heat the oil over medium-low heat, and add the onion. Sauté it for 2 to 3 minutes. Add the mushrooms, season to

taste with salt, and cover the pan. Cook the mushrooms for 15 to 20 minutes, until they are soft.

2. Add the eggs, and cook over low heat, stirring with a wooden spoon, until the eggs are well mixed with the mushrooms and almost set. The dish should be moist and juicy. Serve it immediately, garnished with the parsley.

NOTE: *Do not clean the mushrooms under running water, or they will lose flavor. Instead, wipe them clean with a damp cloth. Break them into small pieces with your fingers.*

Stems of Swiss Chard

❖ PENCAS DE ACELGA ALBARDADAS ❖

Serves 6

In the rural reaches of the Basque Country, Swiss chard is known as *chuletas de la huerta*, which translates as "chops from the vegetable garden." This dish can be served as part of a more elaborate dish, Vegetable Medley (page 54), or as a side dish.

10 Swiss chard stems, white parts only, cut into 2- to 3-inch lengths
¼ cup flour
2 eggs, beaten
½ cup olive oil

1. In a large saucepan, bring about 2 quarts lightly salted water to a boil over high heat. Add the chard, and cook it for about 15 minutes, until it is soft. Drain it well.

2. Spread the flour on a plate, and roll the chard in the flour. Shake off the excess flour. Put the eggs into a shallow bowl.

continued

3. In a skillet, heat the oil over medium-high heat.
4. Dip the chard stems in the egg, and drop them into the oil. Reduce the heat to medium, and cook the chard for about 1 minute. Raise the heat to medium-high, turn the stems, and cook them for about 1 minute longer. Drain them on two layers of paper towels, and serve immediately.

NOTE: *If you like, you can serve the Swiss chard leaves as an accompaniment. Chop them, boil them in salted water, strain them well, and then sauté them in 2 tablespoons olive oil with a sliced clove of garlic.*

Mixed Vegetables with Scrambled Eggs and Ham

• PIPERRADA •

Serves 6

Some of you might recognize this as a French recipe. It's from Iparralde, or "northern Basque country," in Euskera—that is, the French side of the Basque border. I got the recipe from Pierre Henry Guignard, a friend who was posted at the United Nations as a diplomat in the French foreign service. Served with bread, *piperrada* makes a satisfying light meal.

¼ cup plus 2 tablespoons olive oil
½ medium onion, minced
1 garlic clove, whole and unpeeled
5 to 6 large green bell peppers (about 2 pounds), cut into narrow strips
2 pounds tomatoes, diced
3 slices serrano ham or prosciutto, coarsely chopped
6 large eggs, lightly beaten
Salt and fresh-ground black pepper

1. In a skillet, heat the oil over medium heat. Add the onion and garlic, and sauté them for about 5 minutes, until the onion begins to soften. Add the peppers and tomatoes, and sauté them for about 15 minutes longer, until the peppers soften. Remove and discard the garlic clove.
2. Add the ham to the skillet, and sauté for 2 to 3 minutes longer, until the ham is heated through. Add the eggs, and season to taste with salt and pepper. Reduce the heat to low, and, using a wooden spoon, stir the mixture until the eggs are scrambled and smooth. Serve immediately.

Lettuce Hamburgers

❖ LECHUGA ALBARDADA ❖

Makes 8 to 10 patties; serves 4

A delight for vegetarians, these burgers can be eaten alone as a light meal or served as a side dish as well as for a first course. We Basques usually have them as part of a more elaborate dish, Vegetable Medley (page 54). I don't know who first thought of making lettuce patties, but my mother has been making them all my life, and they are lovely.

2 large heads green-leaf, Bibb, or romaine lettuce

¼ cup flour

2 eggs, beaten

½ cup olive oil

1. Remove the thick parts at the base of each lettuce leaf, and chop the remainder of the leaves. In a large saucepan, bring about 2 quarts of lightly salted water to a boil over high heat. Add the lettuce, reduce the heat to medium, and cook the lettuce for about 5 minutes, until it is soft. Drain it until it is nearly dry. Using your fingers, form the lettuce pieces into small balls.

continued

2. Spread the flour on a plate and roll the lettuce balls in the flour, pressing them against the plate to flatten them into patties about 2 inches in diameter. Put the eggs into a shallow bowl.

3. In a large skillet, heat the oil over medium-high heat. Reduce the heat to medium.

4. Dip the lettuce patties in the egg, drop them into the oil, and cook them for about 1 minute. Raise the heat to medium-high, turn the patties, and cook them for about 1 minute longer. Drain them on two layers of paper towels, and serve immediately.

Baked Mushrooms

❖ Setas al Horno ❖

Serves 4 to 6

In the Basque Country we would serve this dish as a first course, with bread that has been fried in olive oil. These mushrooms can also make a lovely accompaniment, however, to grilled or broiled chicken or beef or another main course. Look for fresh, firm mushrooms, each about 2 inches in diameter. Of the mushrooms commonly available in the United States, I prefer shiitakes, for their aroma and subtle flavor. You could substitute another variety, however.

1 pound medium shiitake mushrooms (8 to 10 per person),
wiped clean and stemmed (see Note)
1/2 cup plus 2 tablespoons olive oil
1/2 cup plus 2 tablespoons minced flat-leaf parsley
1/4 cup plus 1 tablespoon minced garlic
Salt

1. Preheat the oven to 500°F. Lightly rub a shallow baking pan with olive oil.
2. Arrange the mushrooms, stem side up, in the baking pan.

3. In a small bowl, whisk together the oil, parsley, and garlic, and season with salt to taste. Spoon some of the mixture onto each mushroom. Bake the mushrooms for about 10 minutes, or until they soften and are lightly browned. Serve immediately.

NOTE: *Wipe the mushrooms clean with a damp cloth; do not rinse them under running water since mushrooms absorb water very easily. Pull or cut off the stems.*

MARICHU: TWO BASQUE RESTAURANTS IN NEW YORK

❧ *My restaurants*, one in Manhattan and the other in Bronxville, New York, are Basque to the core. Both are named Marichu, after my mother, who taught me most of what I know about cooking. I work hard to insure that the food is authentic, prepared much as the food I grew up with was prepared. Many Americans think that Basque food can't be very different from French or Italian food, or even as good. I hope that, by eating at my restaurants and reading this book, Americans will come to recognize Basque culinary traditions as being as distinct and rich as any others. Knowledgeable food lovers throughout Europe, in fact, know that if the phrase *a la vasca* ("in the Basque style") follows a menu offering at a Spanish restaurant, that dish is the best choice for the meal. This is because Basque food, although not always dramatically different from that of surrounding regions, is indisputably the best.

When a customer enters either of the Marichu restaurants, it is my hope that he or she is transported away from New York to northern Spain, where Basque cooks carefully prepare fresh, full-flavored dishes that echo the magnificent food that has been served in the Basque Country for generations. If I stubbornly make only a very few concessions to American palates, it is because I am passionate about the food of my homeland. And it is part of this passion that compels me to open the doors to the restaurants every day to welcome our patrons with the sense of fun, joy, and warmth that defines the Basques.

Green Peas with Ham

• Guisantes con Jamón •

Serves 4

I cannot resist fresh peas when I spy them in the markets in the springtime. My children enjoy shelling them with me, and then we all enjoy this easy side dish. If you add the eggs, it becomes a light supper or lunch. If you cannot find fresh peas, use frozen peas rather than canned. The frozen ones taste better and are more healthful, too, as they retain more vitamins.

2 cups fresh shelled green peas (about 2 pounds in the shells)
or frozen peas
3 tablespoons olive oil
½ medium onion, minced
3 ounces minced serrano ham, prosciutto, or bacon
4 large eggs (optional)

1. In a large saucepan, bring about 6 cups of lightly salted water to a boil, and add the peas. Cook them for about 5 minutes, until they are tender. Drain them well, reserving 1 cup of the cooking liquid.
2. In a skillet, heat the oil over medium heat. Add the onion, and sauté it for about 10 minutes, until it is softened. Add the ham, and, using a wooden spoon, stir to mix well. Add the peas and the reserved cup of cooking liquid, and cook for about 5 minutes, until the peas are heated through and the flavors blended. If you like, add the eggs, sliding them carefully into the pan. Poach them for a few minutes, until they are opaque. Serve immediately in shallow earthenware bowls.

Marichu Salad

❖ ENSALADA MARICHU ❖

Serves 4

Spanish salads, which are always served as a first course (except when a few lettuce leaves accompany roasted lamb), tend to have far more ingredients than appear in most American salads. This dish is a perfect example. It is a salad my mother prepares almost daily in the summertime, for lunch or dinner. It could also be served as a light lunch on its own.

1 head green-leaf lettuce
2 medium tomatoes, cut into 8 wedges each
4 scallions or 1 small onion, chopped
2 boiled small new potatoes, peeled and chopped
1/2 cup small green olives
One 3-ounce can albacore tuna packed in olive oil, flaked with a fork
1/2 cup House Vinaigrette (page 184)
4 canned white asparagus spears, halved crosswise, or
4 cooked fresh white asparagus spears
2 hard-cooked eggs, each cut into 4 wedges

continued

1. Tear the lettuce into large bite-sized pieces, and put them into a large salad bowl. Add the tomatoes, scallions or onion, potatoes, olives, and tuna, and toss well. Add the vinaigrette, and toss well again.
2. Decorate the top of the salad with the asparagus halves and the egg wedges.

NOTES: *I like to soak lettuce in a pan full of water that is mixed with just a drop or two of chlorine bleach. This helps insure that the lettuce is clean. I rinse the lettuce very well, and then spin it dry; moisture on the greens would dilute the flavor of the salad. Also, I never cut lettuce with a knife but instead tear it into pieces.*

The potatoes can be boiled the day before serving. Cook them in lightly salted water for about 20 minutes, until they are fork-tender. Wait until they are cool before peeling and chopping them.

Salad of Mixed Vegetables
❖ ENSALADA DE VERDURAS ❖

Serves 6 to 8

This dish has endless variations, depending on the season and the vegetables that are freshest in the markets and gardens. I prepare this salad in the springtime, when asparagus is harvested and peas and artichokes are especially full-flavored.

FOR THE VEGETABLES:
2 tablespoons or more olive oil
2 large eggplants, sliced crosswise 1 inch thick
Salt
6 artichokes, tough outer leaves and stems discarded, and tips trimmed
Juice of 2 lemons
½ lemon

One 2-pound cauliflower head, separated into florets
2 tablespoons milk
6 small carrots
12 fresh green asparagus spears, trimmed and coarsely chopped
1 cup coarsely chopped string beans
1 cup fresh green peas

FOR THE DRESSING:
½ cup plus 2 tablespoons olive oil
1 garlic clove, minced
1 small onion, minced
6 thin serrano ham or prosciutto slices, minced
2 tablespoons red wine vinegar (optional)

1. To begin preparing the vegetables, heat the olive oil in a skillet or sauté pan over medium-high heat. Add the eggplant slices, and cook them for 1 to 2 minutes on each side, until they are lightly browned (you may have to do this in batches; add more oil as necessary). Sprinkle the slices on both sides with salt, and drain the slices on paper towels.

2. Sprinkle the artichokes with the lemon juice.

3. Fill a large saucepan about halfway with water, and bring the water to a boil over high heat. Add the ½ lemon, a little salt, and the artichokes. Return the water to a boil, reduce the heat, and simmer the artichokes gently for about 30 minutes, until the leaves are easy to remove. Using tongs, lift the artichokes from the water, and drain them. Discard the cooking water.

4. Fill the pan about halfway with more water, and bring it to a boil over high heat. Add the cauliflower and milk, return the liquid to a boil, and reduce the heat. Simmer the cauliflower gently for about 15 minutes, until it is fork-tender. Drain the cauliflower, discarding the cooking liquid.

5. Fill the pan with more water, and bring it to a boil over high heat. Add the carrots, reduce the heat, and cook them slowly for about 15 minutes, until they are tender. Lift them from the water with tongs or a slotted spoon, and drain them. Add the asparagus to the pan, and simmer it for about 15

continued

minutes, until it is tender. Lift it from the water, and drain it. Add the beans, and simmer them for about 10 minutes. Then add the peas, and cook them with the beans for about 15 minutes, until both are done. Drain and discard the water. (You may have to add additional water between vegetables. You may also choose to use more than one pan for cooking the vegetables to make the process go faster.)

6. Arrange the boiled vegetables and the eggplant on a platter. They do not have to be hot but may be warm or at room temperature.

7. To make the dressing, heat the olive oil over medium heat in a skillet, and cook the garlic and onion for about 5 minutes, until the onion is softened. Add the ham, and cook it for 1 to 2 minutes, until it is lightly browned on both sides. Stir well, and then spoon the hot dressing over the vegetables. Sprinkle them with the vinegar, if you like, and serve.

White Asparagus Navarra-Style
❖ ESPÁRRAGOS BLANCOS DE NAVARRA ❖

Serves 4

Anyone who has sampled the canned white asparagus from Navarra, the autonomous community to the east of the Basque Country with which we share a gastronomic heritage, will agree that this asparagus is among the best in the world. As a chef, I nearly always prefer fresh produce to anything canned, but in this instance I demur. The tender, young spears are so good that I serve them regularly at the restaurant. You can substitute fresh white asparagus, of course, just as you can use pimientos instead of the piquillos. Piquillos are mild red peppers, also from Navarra, that are available canned at many specialty-foods shops in the United States.

I always think of my mother when I make the vinaigrette for this dish, not because she invented the dressing but because she prefers it to any other. It goes with many dishes, but none so exquisitely as this one. Keep in mind that the ingredients must be chopped very, very fine, until nearly the size of rice grains. The result, however, is worth the work.

FOR THE VINAIGRETTE:

1 hard-cooked egg, minced very fine
3 piquillo peppers (see Note), minced very fine
3 scallions, white parts only, minced very fine
10 pitted Spanish-style green olives, minced very fine
2 tablespoons sherry vinegar
1/4 cup plus 1 tablespoon extra-virgin olive oil
1 tablespoon minced flat-leaf parsley

FOR THE SALAD:

8 canned piquillo peppers (see Note) or pimientos, cut in half lengthwise
16 canned white asparagus spears, preferably from Navarra, or
cooked fresh white asparagus

. . .

1 tablespoon chopped flat-leaf parsley

1. To prepare the vinaigrette, put the egg, peppers, scallions, olives, vinegar, and parsley into a small bowl, and stir gently to blend them. Add the olive oil in a slow, steady stream, stirring gently. Use the vinaigrette immediately, or cover it and refrigerate it for up to 2 days. Stir it gently before using it.

2. Open out the pepper halves, and arrange four of them in a semicircle on one side of each of four salad plates, so that the tips of the peppers point outward.

3. Cut off the thick bottom third of each asparagus spear, and slice these sections 1/2 inch thick. Lay an asparagus spear on each pepper, so the blunt ends of the spears meet near the edge of the plate and the tips fan outward.

4. Distribute the chopped asparagus at the base of the fan, where the spears meet. Drizzle the vinaigrette on the peppers between the asparagus spears, and garnish with parsley. Serve immediately.

NOTE: *If you can't find piquillo peppers locally, order them from Northern Boulevard (718-779-4971). Northern Boulevard also stocks Navarra canned white asparagus.*

Leeks Vinaigrette

❖ PUERROS A LA VINAGRETA ❖

Serves 4

Leeks, which are mild-flavored non-bulbing onions, are basic to Basque cooking. They show up in numerous recipes and are especially valued from October to early April. They are delicious with a vinaigrette made with sherry vinegar, a very common ingredient in the Basque Country. My mother served this simple salad often when I was growing up.

8 leeks (see below), trimmed and cut into 4- to 6-inch lengths
3 to 4 tablespoons House Vinaigrette (page 184)

In a saucepan, bring about 6 cups of lightly salted water to a boil over high heat. Add the leeks, and cook them for about 30 minutes, until they are tender. Drain them, and transfer them to a platter or shallow bowl. Spoon the vinaigrette over them, and serve them warm, at room temperature, or chilled.

PREPARING LEEKS FOR COOKING

❖ *Leeks can be gritty* if not well cleaned. Slice off the root end, and trim the outer green leaves. Make several slits in the base of the leek, and clean them under cold running water, or let them soak in a sink filled with cold water for at least 10 minutes. Drain the leeks, rinse them again to remove any residual grit, and then cut them as the recipe specifies.

Roasted Red and Green Pepper Salad

✦ Ensalada de Pimientos ✦

Serves 4

Whenever I make this salad, I think of a friend of my parents who tended a large vegetable garden near our summer house at the seashore. When my father caught more squid than we could use, he sent us children into the neighborhood to give them to friends. The gardening enthusiast I remember gave us red and green bell peppers in return, and my mother often made a salad similar to this pretty one.

> *4 red bell peppers, roasted, peeled, and seeded (see page 70)*
> *4 green bell peppers, roasted, peeled, and seeded (see page 70)*
> *4 ounces canned anchovies, drained (see Notes)*
> *House Vinaigrette (page 184)*

1. Tear the roasted peppers in half.
2. On each plate, lay a red pepper half and, next to it, a green pepper half. Top each with a few anchovies, and then lay a pepper half of the opposite color on top. Lay several anchovies on top of the pepper. Repeat this on the other three plates. Spoon a little dressing over the peppers, and serve.

NOTES: *If you can get fresh anchovies marinated in a vinegar brine, use them in place of canned anchovies. Or, if you prefer, substitute dry-cured ham such as serrano or prosciutto for the anchovies.*

    You can, of course, make these stacks of peppers and anchovies higher than two layers by using more peppers or cutting them into smaller pieces.

❧ *I roast peppers* at least once a week at home and daily in the restaurant. Once they are roasted, I store them in a covered container in the refrigerator, where they keep for up to a week. They are the perfect accompaniment for so many foods, including filet mignon, pork chops, pan-fried fish, and even scrambled or fried eggs. The aroma that fills the house when the peppers are roasting is worth the small effort it takes to roast them!

Although I usually roast red bell peppers, you can use this same method to roast other kinds. Begin by wiping the peppers clean with a damp cloth rather than rinsing them under running water; this prevents them from absorbing moisture. Lay them on a baking sheet set on the center rack of the oven, and roast them at 350 degrees for about 1 hour. To keep them from burning, turn them every 15 minutes while they roast, taking care to handle them carefully.

When the peppers are darkened and tender, remove the pan from the oven, and cover the peppers with paper or dish towels (I like to use newspaper). Let the peppers cool until they are tepid, and then peel off the skins. Tear or cut the peppers in half, scrape out the seeds, and collect the juice. Strain the juice, and reserve it. Cut each pepper into strips about 1/3 inch wide or whatever size the recipe calls for.

Although the peppers are ready to use at this point, I prefer to take the extra step of cooking them in olive oil with sliced garlic, salt, and sugar, as we do in the Basque Country. This makes them taste indescribably wonderful. To cook them this way, heat the oil in a skillet over medium heat. Add the garlic, and cook it for 2 to 3 minutes, until it turns golden. Add the peppers, salt and sugar to taste, and the reserved pepper juice. Reduce the heat, and cook the peppers very slowly, stirring often, for about 15 minutes. For eight red bell peppers, I use 1/2 cup plus 2 tablespoons olive oil and one garlic clove. You need only a sprinkling of salt and sugar to bring out the flavor of the peppers.

Hearts of Lettuce Tudela-Style

❖ COGOLLITOS DE TUDELA ❖

Serves 4

Navarra and the Basque Country share similar culinary traditions and attitudes toward food and cooking. For example, Navarra is known for its spectacular vegetables—not just the famed white asparagus and piquillo peppers, but nearly every manner of garden crop. When our friends Patricia and Fernando Abascal were posted in the United States for four years, we spent many happy times together, cooking and eating and discussing the food of our homeland. The Abascals come from a town founded in 802 that is, after Pamplona, the best-known town in Navarra. This salad is typical of Tudela.

8 small heads Bibb lettuce
4 canned piquillo peppers (see Note), canned pimientos, or roasted, peeled, and seeded
fresh red bell peppers (see page 70)
1 garlic clove, minced
1 tablespoon extra-virgin olive oil
16 canned anchovies, drained
1/2 cup House Vinaigrette (page 184)
2 tablespoons chopped flat-leaf parsley

1. Rinse the lettuce heads under cold running water, and drain them until they are dry. Discard the outer leaves, and cut each head in half through the stem.

2. Cut the peppers in half. Unfold the halves, and cut these pieces in half again to make 16 triangular pieces.

3. In a small bowl, whisk together the garlic and olive oil. Spoon the mixture among the leaves of the lettuce halves, taking care that most of the leaves have a little of the mixture clinging to them.

4. Arrange four lettuce halves on each plate. Arrange the pepper triangles on top of each half, and then lay an anchovy fillet on top of each pepper. Drizzle with the vinaigrette, garnish with parsley, and serve.

continued

NOTE: *Piquillo peppers are imported from Navarra and sold in cans or jars. Buy them in specialty-foods stores, or order them from Northern Boulevard (718-779-4971).*

Fresh Tuna Salad with Piquillo Peppers

❖ ENSALADA DE VENTRESCA CON PIQUILLOS ❖

Serves 4

When I arrived in the United States, I was surprised to discover that the most exquisite part of the tuna, the belly (called *ventresca* in Spanish, and actually the breast of the fish), is relatively unknown here. Later, I discovered that the belly is usually sold to the Japanese, who value it for sushi and sashimi. With a little diligence, though, you can buy it from a good fishmonger. This simple salad is made very special indeed by the tender, poached tuna belly, although you can also make it with tuna steak.

¹/₂ pound tuna belly, preferably, or tuna steak
Coarse salt
1 whole garlic bulb (12 to 16 cloves), unpeeled
1 head Bibb or green-leaf lettuce, torn into small pieces
8 canned piquillo peppers (see Note), canned pimientos, or roasted, peeled, and seeded red bell peppers (see page 70), halved lengthwise
¹/₂ cup House Vinaigrette (page 184)
2 tablespoons chopped flat-leaf parsley

1. Sprinkle the tuna with salt, and put the tuna into a pot. Add enough cold water just to cover the tuna, add the garlic bulb, and bring the contents to a boil over medium-high heat. Reduce the heat, and simmer the tuna for about 10 minutes, just until it is opaque throughout. Lift the tuna from the pan, drain the tuna, and discard the cooking water and the garlic.
2. When the tuna is cool enough to handle, separate it into large flakes.
3. Arrange the lettuce around the rim of each plate. Put four pepper halves in the center, unfolded, with the peaks facing outward. Top the peppers with tuna. Drizzle the tuna and the lettuce with the vinaigrette, garnish with parsley, and serve.

NOTE: *Piquillo peppers are imported from Navarra and sold in cans or jars. You can buy them in a specialty-foods store or order them from Northern Boulevard (718-779-4971).*

Salad of Salt Cod with Orange
❖ ENSALADA DE BACALAO CON NARANJA ❖

Serves 4

Salt cod, prepared in endless ways, is served throughout the Basque Country. I learned this simple preparation from Angel Lorente, a chef who has established a reputation for his innovative ways with salt cod. In a wonderful Bilbao shop devoted to salt cod, he now sells all cuts and styles as well as take-out dishes showcasing the fish. I am grateful he shared this delicious recipe with me.

1 pound salt cod, cut into 3-inch-square pieces
About 2 cups milk
½ cup homemade (page 184) or commercial mayonnaise
Juice of ½ orange
¼ cup plus 2 tablespoons extra-virgin olive oil

continued

2 tablespoons cider vinegar
Salt
About 4 cups mixed salad greens, such as
Bibb lettuce, green- and red-leaf lettuce, and cress
1 orange, peeled and sliced into wedges
1 tablespoon chopped flat-leaf parsley

1. Put the fish into a shallow bowl, and cover the fish with cold water. Refrigerate the fish for 24 to 36 hours, changing the water every 8 hours or so. Drain the fish on paper towels, and transfer it to a saucepan.
2. Add enough milk to cover the fish, and heat over medium-high heat until the milk simmers (do not let it boil). Reduce the heat, and simmer the fish gently for 5 to 10 minutes, until it is tender. Drain it, and set it aside to cool.
3. In a small bowl, whisk together the mayonnaise and orange juice, and set the bowl aside.
4. In a separate small bowl, whisk together the olive oil and vinegar. Season the vinaigrette to taste with salt.
5. Put the greens into a bowl, and drizzle them with the vinaigrette. Toss the greens gently, and then arrange them on four salad plates.
6. Carefully remove the skin and bones from the salt cod, and separate the fish into flakes. Top the greens with the salt cod, and spoon the mayonnaise over it. Garnish each plate with orange wedges and parsley, and serve.

Salad of Baby Eels

✦ ENSALADA DE ANGULAS ✦

Serves 4

Baby eels are the most delicate dish I have tasted; when they are in season, in the wintertime, I look forward to them with great anticipation. Because they are scarce, their price has risen to spectacular heights. This explains why they are most often served as a Christmas treat, particularly in my home city of Bilbao. In the

United States baby eels are sold frozen, and the frozen eels are nearly as good as fresh ones. (Never buy them in cans—canned eels are not good at all!) Traditionally baby eels are cooked as *angulas a la cazuela* (page 30), but this salad is becoming popular, too, partly because it requires fewer eels but mostly because it is so tasty.

FOR THE EELS:
2 garlic cloves, peeled and halved
½ pound baby eels (see Notes)
¼ cup plus 1 tablespoon extra-virgin olive oil
1 tablespoon lemon juice
Salt

FOR THE SALAD:
1 head Bibb or green-leaf lettuce
3 tablespoons extra-virgin olive oil
1 tablespoon sherry vinegar

. . .

1 tablespoon chopped flat-leaf parsley

1. To prepare the eels, rub the garlic halves around the side and bottom of a salad bowl. Discard the garlic. Add the eels to the bowl, and gently rub them over the bottom and side of the bowl to absorb some of the flavor of the garlic. Add the oil and lemon juice, season to taste with salt, and mix well.
2. To prepare the salad, whisk together the oil and vinegar in a small bowl, and season the vinaigrette to taste with salt.
3. In a separate bowl, drizzle the vinaigrette over the lettuce, and toss gently. Spoon the lettuce around the rim of each of four salad plates. Arrange the eels in the center of the plates, garnish with parsley, and serve.

NOTES: *If you can't find baby eels locally, you can order them from Northern Boulevard (718-779-4971).*

Defrost frozen eels overnight in the refrigerator. Gently wipe them dry with a kitchen towel, and then refrigerate them, loosely wrapped, until you are ready to cook them or use them in a salad.

BABY EELS, A TREASURE OF THE BASQUE COUNTRY

❧   *Today baby eels* (*angulas*) are three times as costly as when I was a girl, but even then they were an expensive pleasure saved for special occasions. In those days they were less expensive, although still dear, in the French Basque country, and from time to time my father crossed the border to buy some in the town of Hendaye. (Since then the French have discovered the joys of baby eels, and now they are just as expensive in France as they are in Spain). I recall one instance when my mother, planning to serve these treasures for lunch, sent me to the local market for some more, so that we could accommodate some unexpected guests. As I walked home with my precious package, I couldn't resist dipping into the sack to nibble an eel or two. When I arrived at home, my mother was dismayed to discover I had devoured more than half of the eels! She sent someone else back to the market for more—and docked my allowance for several weeks.

When I was first married, before I moved with my husband and children to Madrid, we spent Sundays at my parents' house, where we often had angulas. My very young daughters quickly developed a fondness for the delicacy. After we moved to Madrid, one day my four-year-old daughter, María, and I ran into an acquaintance, a courtly gentleman who insisted that we join him for some refreshment before we went home for lunch. I accepted a small glass of wine, and María, with wide eyes anticipating her treat, asked for the angulas she spied on the counter of the bar where we were seated. I tried to dissuade our friend from ordering them, saying that María had no idea what she was asking for. In fact, I said, she did not even know how angulas taste. "Not so!" exclaimed my daughter. "I have them all the time at my grandmother's." I was embarrassed, but María got her eels and devoured them, clearly loving every bite. To this day I do not want to know what the bill was for that spontaneous, kind invitation.

Larruskain Fish Soup

❖ SOPA DE PESCADO DE LARRUSKAIN ❖

Serves 6

When I was a university student in Bilbao, my friends and I were known to hire a large car or even a bus with a driver to make the trip to a tavern-like restaurant called Txiller in the tiny village of Larruskain—actually only a cluster of a few houses—on the outskirts of Markina, in the province of Vizcaya. We traveled over narrow country roads for more than an hour just so that we could spend an evening there enjoying this wonderful, robust soup and grilled monkfish. It was one of our favorite outings!

Victoria Churruca, Txiller's owner, graciously shared this recipe with me. Larruskain is only a few miles from Ondarroa, a fishing port, which explains the fish and seafood in this soup. For more texture, lay a slice of bread in the bottom of each soup bowl before ladling in the soup.

¹/₂ cup plus 2 tablespoons olive oil

1 small onion, minced

1 small red onion, minced

2 small carrots, julienned

1 leek (see page 68), white part only, minced

continued

1 medium tomato, peeled and diced
½ pound monkfish, cut into small chunks (reserve the bones)
½ pound medium ("U36" or "36-count") shrimp,
peeled and halved crosswise (reserve the peels)
Salt
2 tablespoons unbleached all-purpose flour
½ cup dry white wine
1 pound mussels
½ pound small Manila or littleneck clams (see Note)
A few saffron threads

1. In a large saucepan, heat the olive oil over medium-high heat. Add the onion, carrots, and leek, reduce the heat to low, and sauté the vegetables for about 10 minutes, until they soften. Add the tomato, stir, and simmer for about 5 minutes, until the tomato releases its liquid.

2. While the vegetables cook, sprinkle the monkfish and shrimp with salt. Spread the flour in a shallow bowl, coat the fish and shrimp with the flour, and shake off the excess. Add the fish and shrimp to the pot of vegetables, and cook, stirring, for about 5 minutes. Add the wine, and simmer for 1 to 2 minutes. Remove the pot from the heat.

3. In a large saucepan or stockpot, bring about 6 cups water to a boil over medium-high heat. Add the mussels and clams, and cook them for 3 to 5 minutes, until they open. Lift the clams and mussels from the pan with a slotted spoon, and set them aside. Discard any that have not opened. Add the reserved fish bones and shrimp shells to the cooking liquid. Bring the liquid to a boil over medium-high heat, reduce the heat, and simmer for 15 to 20 minutes.

4. Strain the cooking liquid into another large pot. Add the saffron threads, and season to taste with salt. Add the fish, shrimp, and vegetables from step 2, and the clams and mussels, and bring the soup to a boil. Reduce the heat, and simmer 2 to 3 minutes to blend the flavors. Serve immediately.

NOTE: *A reputable fishmonger should be able to supply you with small, sweet Manila clams, but you may have to call ahead to order them.*

A Word about Cutting Potatoes

◆ *When cutting potatoes* for stews and soups, cut only part of the way into the potato, and then crack or break it the rest of the way. The cracked part will release the potato's starch into the cooking liquid, and the starch will act as a natural thickener. In the Basque Country, this is called an "old grandmother's trick."

Fresh Tuna, Potato, and Green Pepper Stew
◆ Marmitako Arrantzale ◆

Serves 6

The origins of this robust stew lie with the fishermen who made it on their boats when tuna fishing. But in modern times the stew has become an integral part of a summer celebration commemorating the dispute between two coastal Basque villages over the ownership of the tiny island of Izaro, which lies about three kilometers from each village. To settle the dispute, which raged about 150 years ago, the towns organized a rowing race to the island. Now every year on July 22, both villages turn out for a lively regatta that ends in a third coastal town, Elantxobe (a picturesque village built on such a steep hill that donkeys stand on roofs jutting out from the hillside to munch on grass growing on nearby roofs). During the festivities, parties on pleasure boats eat *marmitako* as a tribute to the fishing that has been the mainstay of the region. This pocket of the coast is so rich in sea life and valuable habitats that, in 1989, UNESCO declared it a Protectorate of the Biosphere, an environmentally protected area.

This dish is meant as a first course, but when you increase the amount of water by 1 cup and double the amount of tuna, it becomes a main course.

continued

¹/₂ cup olive oil
1 medium onion, chopped
1 green bell pepper, cut into strips
3 large baking potatoes, peeled and cut into bite-sized chunks
¹/₂ cup Biscayne Sauce (page 187), or 2 tablespoons paprika
3 cups water
1 pound fresh tuna, cut into small chunks
Salt

1. In a stockpot, heat the olive oil over medium heat. Sauté the onion for about 3 minutes, just until it begins to soften. Add the green pepper, and cook for another 3 minutes. Add the potatoes and Biscayne Sauce or paprika, mix well, and then add the water. Bring the mixture to a boil over medium-high heat, stirring now and then, until it boils. Reduce the heat, and cook the stew at a low simmer, uncovered, for about 20 minutes, until the potatoes are fork-tender.

2. Add the tuna to the stew, season to taste with salt, and cook gently for 3 to 4 minutes, just until the tuna is opaque throughout. Transfer the stew to a casserole, and serve.

Leek and Potato Soup

❖ PORRUSALDA ❖

Serves 6

This is a soup typical of the Basque Country, since both leeks and carrots are common vegetables and codfish is the fish of choice for so many meals. When pumpkin is not in season, double the quantity of carrots. The dish traditionally contains salt cod, but over the years I have learned to omit it because my children prefer the soup free of fish. When I know I will be very busy, I double the quantities, and the next day I purée the leftover soup in a blender for another meal.

6 leeks (see page 68), sliced crosswise 1 inch thick
6 large potatoes, peeled and cut into chunks
½ pound fresh pumpkin, peeled and cut into small pieces
1 medium carrot, cut crosswise into 4 or 5 pieces
¼ pound desalted salt cod (optional; see Note), cut into pieces
¼ cup olive oil
Salt

1. In a large saucepan or stockpot, bring 8 cups of lightly salted water to a boil over medium-high heat. Boil the leeks for about 10 minutes, until they are fork-tender.
2. Add the potatoes, pumpkin, carrot, and, if you like, codfish, and boil gently over medium heat for about 20 minutes longer, until the potatoes are tender. Add the oil and salt (be careful with the salt if you are using salt cod), and cook, stirring, for about 1 minute, until the oil is well incorporated. Ladle the soup into shallow soup bowls, and serve.

NOTE: *To reduce the saltiness of salt cod, soak the fish in cold water in the refrigerator for 24 to 36 hours, changing the water about every 8 hours.*

Lentil-Chorizo Soup

❖ SOPA DE LENTEJAS CON CHORIZO ❖

Serves 6

Lentils are included in many Basque dishes, particularly those served during the cold months. When I was growing up, we spent nine months of the year in the capital city of Bilbao, where my six brothers and sisters and I filled the house with noisy activity. As was the custom then, we had domestic help and also a live-in German instructor, which meant that my parents' household included eleven or

continued

twelve persons. The pots and pans in our kitchen were not much smaller than those I have in the restaurants today, and got nearly as much use. Rich, warming soups such as this one were often cooking on the stove.

½ pound brown lentils
3 whole chorizo sausages (about ½ pound; see Notes)
¼ cup plus 2 tablespoons olive oil
3 medium potatoes, peeled and cut into chunks
2 medium carrots, cut into thin rounds
1 green bell pepper, halved and seeded
1 red bell pepper, halved and seeded
1 onion, minced
Salt

1. Put the lentils into a medium flame-proof casserole or other pot, cover them with about 4 cups water, and soak them for about 8 hours.
2. Drain the lentils, and return them to the casserole. Add enough cold water to cover them by 2 to 3 inches. Bring the lentils and water to a boil over medium-high heat, reduce the heat to low, and add the chorizo sausages and 2 tablespoons of the olive oil. Cook the lentils over very low heat for 1 hour.
3. Add the potatoes, carrots, and green and red peppers, and cook for about 20 minutes longer, until the vegetables are fork-tender.
4. In a small skillet, heat the remaining ¼ cup olive oil over medium heat, and cook the onion for 5 to 10 minutes, stirring, until it is softened. Add the onion and oil to the soup, mix well, and cook for about 10 minutes, until the flavors blend. Cut each chorizo in half, and serve 1 piece to a bowl. Season to taste with salt, and serve.

NOTES: *Excellent Spanish chorizo is available from Northern Boulevard (718-779-4971).*

Purée leftover soup in a food processor or blender, and serve it hot, topped with croutons. Because lentils are rich in iron, this is a good soup for children.

Onion Soup Basque-Style

❧ SOPA KIPULA AL IDIAZABAL ❧

Serves 6

The special flavor and texture of Spanish Basque onion soup comes from aged Idiazabal, a sheep's milk cheese that is smoked over hardwood fires (see page 84). If you can't find aged Idiazabal, however, you can use Gruyère cheese, as the French Basques do.

¹/₄ cup olive oil
1 tablespoon unsalted butter
4 onions, sliced lengthwise
4 cups homemade (pages 194–96) or canned beef or chicken broth
(see Note)
Salt
12 thin slices white bread
³/₄ cup grated aged Idiazabal or Gruyère cheese (page 84)

1. In a large pot, heat the oil and butter over medium heat. Sauté the onions for 20 to 30 minutes, until they are soft.
2. Add the broth, bring it to a simmer, and cook the soup for about 10 minutes longer, until it is hot and the liquid is infused with the onions. Season the soup to taste with salt.
3. Lay two slices of bread in the bottom of each of four shallow soup plates, and sprinkle each serving with 3 tablespoons of the cheese. Ladle the soup over the bread and cheese, and serve immediately.

NOTE: *For this and many soups I use homemade broth (for others I create the broth while making the soup). But many canned broths are quite good and can be substituted for homemade, although they will never have the same depth of flavor.*

❧ *In the mountains* and valleys in and near the Basque Country, the climate is perfect for raising healthy cows, goats, and sheep, all of which produce rich, creamy milk. From this milk Spain produces some exceptional cheeses. The most celebrated of the Basque cheeses is Idiazabal, a smoked sheep's milk cheese. It has become a great favorite not only in its region of origin but throughout the rest of Spain and much of Europe, and exports to the United States and elsewhere are growing. Basques themselves are so crazy about this cheese that they hold contests to match artisan cheesemakers against each other. Recently, a prize-winning wheel of Idiazabal cheese was auctioned at the Ordizia market (near Tolosa) for about five thousand dollars.

The handmade cheese is encased in a hard, dark brown, inedible rind. After a few months' aging, the cheese inside is light-colored with a lovely buttery, nutty flavor. When aged for a long period, Idiazabal cheese becomes firm, dry, and sharp—perfect for grating for Onion Soup Basque-Style.

If you can't find Idiazabal cheese locally, order it from Northern Boulevard (718-779-4971).

Red-Bean Stew Tolosa-Style

✦ ALUBIAS ROJAS DE TOLOSA ✦

Serves 8

The good cooks of Tolosa have long been famous for the red-bean stews they make in this market town in Guipúzcoa, the Basque province closest to France. Tolosa, where the familiar Basque berets are manufactured, is less than 20 miles from San Sebastián (Donostia, in Euskera), and is also home to an impressive confectionary museum, which contains candy-making equipment and utensils dating to the fifteenth century. Nestled in a river valley, the town hosts a wonderful farmers' market in the square every Saturday.

Although there may be as many variations of this dish as there are cooks in town, the recipe here is representative of the region's stews. If you travel to Tolosa, try the outstanding version served at Herriko Etxea, a tavern in the nearby village of Albiztu. As elsewhere in Tolosa, the stew is served with spicy, hot pickled green peppers called *guindillas*.

I like to make this on cold winter weekends, when I have the three hours necessary for its preparation. The stew is great for family meals, but it is also a tasty and convenient dish for casual entertaining; make it in the morning and reheat it when your guests arrive.

2 pounds dried red beans
1 leek (see page 68), cut into 2 or 3 pieces
1 medium carrot, cut into 2 or 3 pieces
1 medium onion
8 whole small chorizo sausages (about 1¼ pounds; see Notes)
4 whole blood sausages (about ¾ pound; optional; see Notes)
¼ cup olive oil
1 tablespoon paprika
Salt

continued

1. In a large pot or bowl, combine the beans with enough cold water to cover them by 1 to 2 inches. Soak the beans for 8 to 10 hours. Drain them, and transfer them to a stockpot.

2. Add to the pot the leek, the carrot, and half the onion, in one piece, and then add enough cold water to cover the vegetables by 2 to 3 inches. Bring the contents to a boil over high heat, and cook rapidly for 2 to 3 minutes, skimming any foam from the surface. Reduce the heat, and simmer the beans gently for about 1½ hours, until they are fork-tender.

3. Add the chorizo sausages, and cook for about 1 hour longer, until the sausage is tender.

4. If you're using the blood sausages, put them into a saucepan, and add enough cold water to barely cover them. Cook them over medium heat for about 30 minutes, until they are tender, adding more water as necessary. Drain them, and set them aside.

5. In a skillet, heat the olive oil over medium-high heat. Chop the remaining onion half, and add the onion and paprika to the skillet. Sauté for about 5 minutes, until the onion is soft. Purée the mixture in a food mill or blender. Add the purée to the soup, and season the soup to taste with salt. If you prefer, remove the onion half, the leeks, and the carrot.

6. Heat the soup through, and add the blood sausage, if you're using it. Ladle the soup into shallow bowls, and serve it immediately, making sure that each serving contains a chorizo sausage and half a blood sausage.

NOTES: *Excellent Spanish chorizo and blood sausage are available from Northern Boulevard (718-779-4971).*

I like to purée any leftover soup in a blender or food processor, heat it gently, and serve it hot, topped with croutons.

The Indispensable Food Mill

❧ *Food mills play a major role* in Basque kitchens, and I think it's a shame that they aren't more popular in the United States. Because these inexpensive tools are helpful for many kitchen tasks, I frequently suggest that you use one. When food is passed through a food mill, all skins and seeds are extracted and lumps are smoothed out, although the mill never purées food to the degree that a blender or food processor does. This is precisely what I like about food mills. The food comes out more textured, and it keeps its color instead of turning lighter, as often happens when food is pulverized in one of the more powerful machines.

Sold at kitchenware and general houseware stores, food mills are hand-cranked sieves with perforated bottoms; some come with exchangeable base plates with perforations of different sizes. Some mills also have brackets for hooking them onto the edges of pans and bowls. Most mills hold between 2 and 3½ quarts. Once you begin using a food mill, you too will find it indispensable.

White-Bean Stew

Serves 8

This warm and filling stew is a typical winter dish in the Basque Country. In the Asturias region of Spain, cooks mix this stew with clams in *salsa verde* (page 143) to make an even more robust dish called *Fabes con Almejas*.

2 pounds dried white beans
1 leek (see page 68), halved lengthwise
1 green bell pepper, halved and seeded
1 red bell pepper, halved and seeded
¼ cup olive oil
1 small onion, chopped
1 tablespoon paprika
Salt

1. In a large pot or bowl, combine the beans with enough cold water to cover them by 1 to 2 inches. Soak the beans for at least 8 hours. Drain them, and transfer them to a stockpot.

2. Add the leek and peppers to the pot, and then add enough cold water to cover the vegetables by 2 to 3 inches. Bring the contents to a boil over high heat, and cook rapidly for 2 to 3 minutes, skimming any foam from the surface. Reduce the heat, and simmer gently for about 2 hours, adding about ¼ cup cold water to the pot every 30 minutes (this softens the beans). The beans are done when they are fork-tender.

3. In a skillet, heat the olive oil over medium-high heat. Add the onion, and sauté for about 10 minutes, until the onion is soft. Add the paprika, and cook, stirring, for about 2 minutes longer, until the mixture is well blended. Add it to the beans.

4. Remove the leek and peppers from the beans, if you prefer, and discard them. Season the stew to taste with salt. Reheat the stew gently, if necessary. Ladle it into shallow soup bowls, and serve.

Garlic and Bread Soup

◆ SOPA DE AJO ◆

This recipe reflects the humble and ancient culinary roots so apparent in the Basque Country. In frugal kitchens, it was considered wasteful to discard even a handful of bread crumbs, and so soups such as this one were developed as a way to use every bit of food in the larder. Many Basque recipes are born of similar circumstances, and I thank my ancestors for their common sense, care, and great sense of flavor and texture. This soup is truly satisfying and comforting, although it is a homely looking brew.

¹/₂ cup olive oil
6 garlic cloves, sliced thin
¹/₂ slightly stale baguette, sliced thin (see Note)
1 tablespoon paprika
4 cups water or homemade (page 194) or commercial chicken broth
Salt
1 teaspoon hot red pepper flakes (optional)
6 large eggs

1. In a clay or other flame-proof casserole or skillet, heat the olive oil over medium heat. Add the garlic, and fry it, stirring with a wooden spoon, for 2 to 3 minutes, until it is golden. Take care the garlic does not burn.

2. Add the bread, and turn it several times so that it absorbs the oil. Sprinkle it with the paprika, and toss well. Add the water or broth, and cook for 10 to 15 minutes, stirring, until the soup is heated through and well blended and the bread has absorbed much of the liquid. Season to taste with salt and, if you like, the pepper flakes.

3. Just before serving the soup, crack the eggs, and slide them onto the surface of the soup, taking care not to break the yolks. Let the eggs cook for 1

continued

to 2 minutes, until the whites are set. Serve the soup by spooning it gently into shallow bowls, allowing one egg per serving.

NOTE: *Use a slender, European-style baguette. A half baguette is 10 to 12 inches long. Traditionally, the baguette should be a day old.*

Potato and Chorizo Stew Rioja-Style

❖ PATATAS A LA RIOJANA ❖

Serves 6

The French chef Paul Bocuse was asked to prepare a meal for the hundredth anniversary of the Bodegas Cune winery in the Rioja region of Spain, which borders the Basque Country and shares many of its traditions. When he visited the kitchen, the esteemed chef sampled this simple potato stew, which the winery's cook had prepared for her own supper. He was so delighted with the stew, he reportedly announced to the winery's owners that they had no need for his food when they had such a treasure right before them! I share Chef Bocuse's enthusiasm for this earthy and very easy dish. Try it with a glass of smooth Rioja red wine.

¼ cup plus 2 tablespoons olive oil

1 medium onion, minced

*2 chorizo sausages (about 5 ounces), removed from their casings and diced
(see Notes)*

*5 medium baking potatoes (about 2½ pounds),
peeled and cut into 1-inch chunks (see Notes)*

1 tablespoon hot paprika

1½ teaspoons salt

6 cups water

1. In a stockpot or other large pot, heat the oil over medium heat. Add the onion, and cook it for about 5 minutes, until it is softened. Add the sausage, and cook, stirring, for about 1 minute, or just until the meat begins to brown.

2. Add the potatoes, paprika, and salt, and stir well. Add the water, increase the heat, and bring the contents to a boil. (Add a little more water, at least enough to cover the potatoes by 1 inch, if you prefer the stew more soupy.) Reduce the heat to medium-low, cover the pot, and simmer gently for about 30 minutes, until the potatoes are tender. Ladle the stew into shallow bowls, and serve.

NOTES: *The original recipe calls for "chestnut-size" pieces of potato. It's important to use starchy potatoes, such as russets, since the potato starch is the only thickener. To ensure a thick stew, also, see "A Word about Cutting Potatoes" on page 79. If the stew seems to need a little extra thickening, crush a few potatoes against the side of the pot before serving.*

Excellent Spanish chorizo is available from Northern Boulevard (718-779-4971).

Chickpeas and Beef Shanks with Cabbage

❖ COCIDO DE GARBANZOS ❖

Serves 12

My mother made this thrifty, hearty meal on many winter Sundays. Although time-consuming to prepare, the dish is worth the effort because it is an entire meal: You serve the broth as soup for a first course, and then the rest of the ingredients on a platter for the main course. Save this recipe for when you're feeding a small crowd, or plan to have plenty of leftovers.

continued

When I was a girl, the bone marrow, served separately, caused many disputes at the table—there was never enough to satisfy us! I have made the bones optional here, however, because so many of us have gotten out of the habit of cooking with them.

1 pound dried chickpeas
One 1-pound ham bone (optional)
12 small marrow bones wrapped in cheesecloth (optional)
4 pounds beef shank
6 chicken legs
12 leeks (see page 68), cut crosswise into 4 pieces
1 bunch flat-leaf parsley
Salt
8 quarts water
1 pound chorizo sausage (about 6 small sausages)
6 medium carrots
6 small red potatoes, peeled
4 pounds cabbage, minced
1/4 cup plus 1 tablespoon olive oil
3 garlic cloves, sliced thin
8 ounces pasta shells or twists
1 quart Tomato Sauce (page 186), warmed

1. To prepare the chickpeas, put them into a large pot or bowl with enough cold water to cover them by 1 to 2 inches. Soak them for at least 8 hours. Drain them, then wrap the soaked chickpeas in a double layer of cheesecloth. Tie the cheesecloth closed with a piece of kitchen twine.

2. In a large stockpot, combine the chickpeas, in the cheesecloth; the ham bone and marrow bones, if you're using them; the beef shanks, chicken legs, leeks, and parsley; salt to taste; and 5 quarts water. Bring the contents to a boil over high heat. Reduce the heat, and simmer gently for about 2½ hours. Several times during the simmering, skim the foam that rises to the surface.

3. Add the chorizos, carrots, and potatoes to the stockpot, and simmer gently for about 1 hour longer, until the vegetables are very soft and the meat is thoroughly cooked.

4. While the meat and vegetables cook, prepare the cabbage. Bring 3 quarts water to a boil in a large saucepan or stockpot. Add the cabbage and salt, and boil for about 30 minutes, or until the cabbage is very soft. Drain it thoroughly.

5. In a large skillet, heat the oil over medium heat. Add the garlic and, when it is golden, the cabbage. Cook them, stirring, for about 10 minutes, until the flavors blend. Remove the skillet from the heat.

6. Strain the broth from the meat, bones, and vegetables, and transfer the broth to a large saucepan or another stockpot. Add the pasta, and bring the broth to a boil over high heat. Cook the pasta for about 15 minutes, until it is tender.

7. While the pasta cooks, shred the meat from the beef shanks and the chicken legs, and arrange the meat on a serving platter. Cut the sausages, carrots, and potatoes into pieces, and arrange them on the platter, too. Discard the leeks, parsley, and ham bone.

8. If you like, scrape the marrow from the marrow bones, and put it into a small dish. Discard the bones.

9. Unwrap the chickpeas, and transfer them to a serving bowl. Cover the bowl, and keep the chickpeas warm.

10. Reheat the cabbage in the skillet over medium heat. When the cabbage is hot, arrange it on the platter so that it surrounds the rest of the food.

11. Serve the pasta and broth as soup, then serve the meat and vegetables as the main course. Accompany the meat and vegetables with the Tomato Sauce, the chickpeas, and, if you like, the marrow.

NOTES: *Boiling the cabbage for 30 minutes may seem excessive to Americans, but Basques like cabbage this way.*

If you like, toss the Tomato Sauce with the shredded meat rather than passing the sauce separately.

Navarran White Asparagus Cream Soup

❖ CREMA DE ESPÁRRAGOS DE NAVARRA ❖

Serves 8

The Navarrans are well known for their expertise with canned foods, including sweet, tender white asparagus as well as piquillo peppers. There's a joke going around my hometown that two gentlemen from Navarra, upon first encountering the dramatic building for the new Guggenheim Museum in Bilbao, wondered aloud about the size and number of asparagus spears it would take to fill the gigantic "can." In my cooking I generally use fresh vegetables, but when it comes to asparagus, I turn to Navarra's canned white spears.

If you can't find Navarra canned white asparagus locally, you can order it from Northern Boulevard (718-779-4971), a store in Queens, New York. Or use other high-quality canned white asparagus or fresh white asparagus; you'll need about 21 spears.

½ cup olive oil
1 medium onion, chopped
Three 12-ounce cans white asparagus, preferably from Navarra,
each spear cut crosswise into 5 pieces (reserve 1 cup canning brine)
2 cups homemade (page 194) or commercial chicken broth
1½ cups heavy cream
Salt
Snipped chives

1. In a large saucepan, heat the oil over medium heat. Add the onion, and sauté it for about 5 minutes, until it is softened. Set the asparagus tips aside, and mix the remaining asparagus well with the onion. Add the 1 cup canning liquid and the broth, and bring the mixture to a boil over medium-high heat. Reduce the heat, and simmer for about 30 minutes, to blend the flavors.

2. Add the cream, and simmer for about 10 minutes longer, taking care not to let the cream boil. Season to taste with salt. Transfer the mixture to a blender or food processor, and blend it nearly to a purée (you may have to do this in batches). Pour the soup through a fine-mesh strainer, and serve it warm, garnished with chives and the reserved asparagus tips.

THE GUGGENHEIM IN BILBAO

❧ *One of the architectural masterworks* of the late twentieth century is the Guggenheim Bilbao Museum, which opened its doors to the public in October of 1997. The museum continues the Solomon R. Guggenheim Foundation's tradition of combining excellence in art with excellence in architecture, a concept realized when Frank Lloyd Wright designed the world-famous Guggenheim Museum on Fifth Avenue in New York City. Frank O. Gehry continued this tradition with his design for the striking museum now standing in Bilbao.

The sober, square stone administration building contrasts sharply with the mammoth glass walls and curved, titanium-covered shapes of the structure that houses the works of art. Inside, the collection consists mainly of works by the most prominent artists of the past half century, but it also includes classic works by Chagall, Kandinsky, Matisse, and Picasso. Having invigorated Bilbao far beyond any predictions, the museum makes a trip to the city more appealing than ever.

Puréed Mixed Vegetable Soup

✦ Puré de Verduras ✦

Serves 6

In Spain we use a lot of purées; they are a delicious way to turn an ordinary preparation into an interesting one. I rarely bought commercially prepared baby food for my four children; instead I fed them fresh purées. This purée is a far cry from baby food, but it will soothe your soul nonetheless. I like it with croutons.

4 medium potatoes, cut into chunks
2 leeks (see page 68), both white and green parts, cut crosswise into 4 or
5 pieces
2 medium carrots, cut into chunks
1 bunch spinach (see Note)
6 cups water
3 tablespoons olive oil
Salt

1. In a large saucepan or stockpot, combine the potatoes, leeks, carrots, and spinach with the water, and bring the contents to a boil over high heat. Reduce the heat, and simmer gently for about 30 minutes, until the potatoes, leeks, and carrots are fork-tender. Add the oil, and season to taste with salt. Cook for about 5 minutes longer so the flavors blend.

2. Purée the mixture in a blender, food processor, or food mill (you may have to do this in batches). Return the purée to the pot, and gently heat it, if necessary. Ladle it into shallow soup bowls, and serve.

NOTE: *Spinach needs very thorough washing to rid the leaves of mud and sand. Break off the toughest, thickest stems, and then submerge the spinach in a pan or sink filled with cool water. Swish the spinach gently in the water, and let it soak for about 10 minutes. Lift the spinach from the water, transfer it to a large colander, and rinse the spinach under cool running water. Shake the colander gently. There is no need to dry the leaves thoroughly for this recipe.*

Main Courses

When I was a 20-year-old student, weighing about 100 pounds, I could eat a three-pound steak without blinking an eye. Now I am more moderate in my consumption of red meat, but the fact remains that we Basques adore oversized steaks. They are commonly prepared in txokos, our famed gastronomic societies, and in asadores (grill houses), as are other charcoal-grilled and pan-cooked meats. As soon as the huge steaks are lifted from the heat, they are sprinkled with coarse sea salt, *which makes them especially delicious. Although beef is the Basque favorite, we like other red meats, too. Our sheep farmers breed their flocks all year long so that we have tender lamb whenever we want it. Still, the best lamb seems to be available in the spring, and I can think of no better meal than one of sweet, tender, almost-white young lamb. For my restaurants, a Basque farmer in upstate New York supplies me with very young lamb year round. Basques also like pork, so here you will find recipes for pork loin, fresh ham, and even young suckling pig, a typically Castillian treat loved by Basques. Since we are great hunters and sportsmen, we are also fond of venison, and so I have included a recipe that in Spain we prepare with roe deer. Roe deer is not available in the United States, but any venison works well. And because we Basques frequently eat organ meats, such as brains, kidneys, tripe, and liver, I have included a recipe for lamb liver and another for veal kidneys just to give you a taste of how delicious these cuts can be.*

We eat as much chicken as we do any other meat. Although the Basques are subjected to mass-produced, plastic-wrapped supermarket chickens just as is anyone in the industrialized world, we fortunately have good access to free-range poultry. Usually a short drive into the countryside is all that's needed to find a farmer raising and selling free-range chickens. They are be-

coming increasingly easy to find in the United States, too, in butcher shops and even supermarkets, and I highly recommend that you try them. No chicken tastes better than a happy hen, who has been permitted to scratch for her food and exercise her muscles in a farmyard.

Basques also enjoy other poultry, as well as game birds such as quail and pheasant. I include a recipe for duck, which Basques have eaten for generations. Although my mother rarely cooked it when I was growing up, duck is now quite fashionable in the Basque Country.

Fish is integral to the Basque diet. Whether rich or poor, we Basques buy the best fresh fish that we can. Because lunch tends to be the larger of our two main meals, we usually choose lighter fare for dinner, which often means fish—but sometimes we eat fish at both meals. We insist on only one thing: that the fish be as fresh as possible. Of course, there is one notable exception to this caveat, and that is salt cod. Basques love it. I have included quite a few recipes for salt cod (as well as for fresh cod), since without it a Basque's culinary life would be bereft indeed.

As you will find as you read the notes preceding the recipes in this chapter, when I was young my family was one of avid sports fishermen. In the summer, my father and brothers spent hours on the sea, fishing for everything with fins or tentacles. And my mother cooked it all, much to our joy then and my continued delight now. Most of the preparations included here are hers. The method I use to sauté hake and scrod fillets might seem unusual to the uninitiated, but I hope you will try it. Whisking the egg whites just until they are opaque and beginning to thicken (the snow point, I call it), aerates them just enough so that they coat the fish with a lovely, light, and gently puffed exterior.

Basques are not inclined to buy fish wrapped in plastic at the supermarket. We prefer to smell the faint brininess of fresh fish and see their clear eyes and firm scales. In the Basque Country, all types of fish and shellfish are sold in small markets and in large market halls, beautifully displayed on chipped ice. As has been the tradition for centuries, the selling stalls are run by women, because the men are out at sea on their boats, catching fish for the next day's meals. (No one buys fish on Monday since Sunday is the fishermen's day of rest.) If you travel to Bilbao, be sure to visit the Mercado de la Ribera, the large multilevel market selling produce on one floor, meat and poultry on another, and fish on a third. A spectacular feast for the senses, it will provide the casual visitor with a good overview of our favorite foods.

Grilled Filet Mignon with Roasted Red Peppers

◆ SOLOMILLO DE BUEY CON PIMIENTOS ROJOS ◆

Serves 4

Although we Basques consume a staggering variety of fish and seafood, we love meat. Most Basque chefs seem to prefer the bolder-flavored sirloin steaks or large T-bones, but for this recipe I like the delicate flavor and tenderness of filet mignon. You can substitute whatever cut of steak you prefer.

6 tablespoons olive oil, plus a little more
1 garlic clove, sliced
2 roasted red bell peppers (see page 70), cut into 1/4-inch-wide strips
1/2 teaspoon sugar, or more, to taste
Coarse salt
Four 4-ounce filets mignons

1. In a skillet, heat 6 tablespoons olive oil over medium heat. Add the garlic, and cook it for about 1 minute, until it is golden. Add the roasted peppers, the sugar, and ½ to 1 teaspoon salt. Cook slowly, stirring, for about 10 minutes, until the flavors blend. Cover the pan, and keep the peppers hot.
2. Prepare a charcoal or gas grill, or heat a skillet until it is searing hot.
3. Rub both sides of each steak with olive oil. Grill or pan-sear the steaks for 3 to 4 minutes per side, until they are as done as you like. Sprinkle a little coarse salt on the steaks after turning them. When they are done, invert them, salted-side down, onto plates, and sprinkle the steaks with a little more salt. Serve them with the peppers.

NOTE: *If you are grilling outdoors, I suggest using a gas grill with lava rocks to better control the heat. Soak some wood chips in water for about 30 minutes, and sprinkle them over the fire to add subtle flavor to the steak.*

THE BASQUES AND STEAK

❧ *As you can* tell from the amounts of meat I call for in the recipes, we Basques truly love steak. When I am in the Basque Country and I crave a great steak, particularly a T-bone, I visit Etxebarri, a restaurant owned by my friend Bittor Arginzoniz and situated in Axpe-Marzana, a town about 30 minutes from Bilbao. The steaks there are better than any I can get in New York steak houses. Perhaps this is because steaks as well as other juicy cuts of meat have always been popular in the *txokos*, the gastronomic societies in which Basque men have passed on culinary skills from one generation to another.

Sirloin Steak with Idiazabal Cheese Sauce

◆ CHULETÓN AL IDIAZABAL ◆

Serves 4

In this wonderfully indulgent recipe, steak is made divine by a sauce of Idiazabal cheese. This justly acclaimed Basque sheep's milk smoked cheese has a lovely texture, buttery, nutty flavor, and firm rind.

Before pan-frying the steaks, be sure to rub salt into them. As a rule, salting meat before cooking it is not a good idea because the salt draws the juices from the meat. In this case, though, the meat juices marry with the cheese and cream to make the simple yet glorious sauce.

3 tablespoons olive oil
Four 8- to 10-ounce sirloin steaks
Salt
4 ounces Idiazabal cheese, cut into small chunks (see Note)
³/₄ cup heavy cream

1. In a large skillet, heat the olive oil over high heat.
2. While the oil heats, sprinkle the steaks lightly with salt, and rub the salt into the meat. Lay a steak in the hot oil, and cook it for 30 seconds on each side for rare meat, longer if you like it better done. Lift the steak from the pan, lay it on a heated plate, and keep it warm while you cook the remaining steaks.
3. Reduce the heat to medium, and add the cheese to the skillet. Using a wooden spoon, stir until the cheese begins to soften and melt. Stir in the cream, and whisk it with the cheese. Raise the heat, and bring the sauce to a boil. Cook it, stirring, for 2 to 3 minutes longer, until the sauce begins to thicken and turn light golden brown. Spoon the sauce over each steak, and serve immediately.

NOTE: *If you cannot find Idiazabal cheese, substitute Cabrales or a good Gorgonzola, even though Idiazabal is not a blue-veined cheese. For more on Idiazabal cheese, see page 84.*

Beef Shanks Marichu-Style

❖ ZANCARRÓN MARICHU ❖

Serves 6

When I was young, my mother prepared this dish at least once a week. We children never tired of it—and when I became a mother I discovered why she had made it so often: It is easy, inexpensive, and convenient, and the shank meat is deliciously tender. This dish is a good candidate for advance preparation: Prepare it in the morning or the day before serving, and reheat it just before dinner. I also like it for large gatherings, and I nearly always serve it with Basque Fries (page 198).

2 pounds beef shanks

Salt

3 tablespoons unbleached all-purpose flour

1/4 cup plus 2 tablespoons olive oil

2 medium onions, chopped

1 garlic clove, chopped

1 medium carrot, sliced thin

1 cup homemade (page 195) or commercial beef broth

1/4 cup Spanish sherry

1. Using a large, sharp knife, cut the shanks into 1 1/2- to 2-inch lengths. Sprinkle them lightly with salt. Spread the flour on a plate, and coat the shank pieces with it. Shake off the excess flour.

2. In a large skillet, heat the oil over high heat. Add the shanks, and sauté them for about 10 minutes, turning them frequently, until they are golden brown. Lift them from the pan with a slotted spoon or tongs, and set them aside.

3. Add the onions and garlic to the skillet, and sauté them for about 10 minutes over medium heat, until the onions begin to soften. Add the carrot,

continued

and cook for about 10 minutes longer, until the carrot softens and the onions brown. Take care that they do not burn.

4. Return the shanks to the pan, add the broth and sherry, and cover the pan. Cook the shanks over medium-low heat for 45 minutes to 1 hour, or until the meat is tender.

5. Lift the shanks from the pan. Transfer the sauce in the pan to a food mill, blender, or food processor, and purée the sauce. Put the shanks into a casserole and top with the sauce. Serve the shanks immediately, or refrigerate them. Reheat them over medium heat.

Oxtails Bilbao-Style

❖ RABO DE BUEY ASTE NAGUSIA ❖

Serves 4

A friend of mine prepared this outstanding dish for one of the cooking contests held during Bilbao's Semana Grande, or Aste Nagusia. Although my friend used the tails of slain fighting bulls, I have substituted oxtails.

4 pounds oxtails, cut into pieces
Salt
About 3 tablespoons unbleached all-purpose flour
$\frac{1}{2}$ cup olive oil
1 medium onion, chopped
2 medium carrots, chopped
2 medium tomatoes, diced
2 leeks (see page 68), chopped
2 garlic cloves, chopped
One 750-milliliter bottle (about 3 cups) red Rioja wine
2 cups water

1. Sprinkle the oxtails with the salt.
2. Spread the flour in a shallow dish, and coat the oxtails on all sides. Shake off the excess flour.
3. In a large, deep skillet or a pot, heat the oil over medium heat. Cook the oxtails for 4 to 5 minutes, until they are golden brown on all sides. Add the onion, carrots, tomatoes, leeks, and garlic, and stir. Cook, stirring, for about 10 minutes, until the vegetables begin to soften.
4. Add the wine and water, and reduce the heat. Cook for about 2½ hours, until the oxtails are tender. Lift the oxtails from the pan, arrange them on a platter, and cover them to keep them warm.
5. Transfer the contents of the pan to a food mill, blender, or food processor, and purée them. Spoon the sauce over the oxtails, and serve.

BILBAO'S ANNUAL FESTIVAL

❧ *Called La Semana Grande* or Aste Nagusia, Bilbao's annual festival begins on the first Saturday after August 15 and continues for a riotous week. Similar to the world-famous festival in Pamplona, our celebration includes bull fighting, street parties, and opera performances. Because we are a people who love to cook and eat, cooking contests figure prominently in the festivities. The contests are usually held right on the street, with makeshift grills and long tables, and everyone who happens by acts the role of critic. Local butchers sell parts of the slain bulls not usually available, such as the tail, from which we make stew. During other times of the year, we make oxtail stew.

Venison with Red Currant Sauce

◆ VENADO CON SALSA DE GROSELLA ◆

Serves 6

Since my father and brothers hunted deer every fall (usually in the Picos de Europa, mountains in Asturias) I grew up enjoying venison. When I moved to the United States, I was pleasantly surprised to discover that I could buy venison in butcher shops and many supermarkets. You can also order it by phone, from D'Artagnan (800-DARTAGNAN or 973-344-0565). If you like game meat, you will love this dish.

FOR THE VENISON:

2 tablespoons olive oil

1 tablespoon dried thyme leaves

1 tablespoon chopped flat-leaf parsley

2 bay leaves, minced or crumbled

Salt and fresh-ground black pepper

4 pounds venison tenderloin or sirloin

FOR THE SAUCE:

¼ cup olive oil

1 large onion, chopped

1 garlic clove, chopped

2 teaspoons dried thyme leaves

1 tablespoon chopped flat-leaf parsley

10 bay leaves, minced or crumbled

1 cup red Rioja wine

½ cup brandy or cognac

¼ cup red currant jelly

Salt and fresh-ground black pepper

1½ teaspoons cornstarch, mixed with 2 tablespoons water (optional)

1. Cut 5 ounces of tips from the venison, and reserve them for the sauce. To prepare the rest of the venison, mix the oil, thyme, parsley, and bay leaves to a paste in a small bowl. Season to taste with salt and pepper, and then rub the paste onto the meat. Put the meat into a shallow glass or ceramic dish, cover the dish, and refrigerate it for 3 to 8 hours.

2. To prepare the sauce, heat the oil over medium heat in a deep skillet or a pot. Add the onion, garlic, thyme, parsley, and bay leaves, and sauté them for 5 to 10 minutes, until the onions soften. Add the venison tips, and sauté for about 5 minutes longer, until the meat begins to brown. Add the wine, and cook, uncovered, for about 15 minutes, until the meat is cooked through.

3. Transfer the meat and wine mixture to a food mill, and press the mixture firmly to extract as much sauce as possible. Alternatively, purée the mixture in a food processor or blender. Return the sauce to the skillet, add the brandy or cognac and the jelly, and season to taste with salt and pepper. Cook, stirring, over medium heat for about 5 minutes. For a thicker consistency, stir the cornstarch mixture into the sauce. Cover the skillet, and keep the sauce warm.

4. Prepare a charcoal or gas grill, or preheat a skillet over medium-high heat.

5. Using a knife, scrape the herb mixture off the venison. Cut the meat into 1½-inch-thick medallions, and season them to taste with salt and pepper. Grill or pan-sear them for 1 to 2 minutes on each side for rare meat. For medium-rare to medium, cook the meat for 5 to 7 minutes per side. Reheat the sauce gently, if necessary, while the meat cooks. Serve the meat immediately on heated plates with the sauce spooned over.

Braised Rabbit in Red Rioja Wine Sauce

❖ CONEJO GUISADO ❖

Serves 4

Apopular saying in the Basque Country is *"El conejo por San Juan y la perdiz por Navidad,"* or "Rabbit on Saint John's day (June 24) and partridge on Christmas." Although we do follow these traditions, we actually eat rabbit all year round. Rabbits arrived on the Iberian Peninsula from Asia twelve centuries ago, and ever since we have enjoyed them prepared in numerous ways. Rabbit has only about 5 percent fat, which makes it a healthful meat that many compare to chicken. Try rabbit cooked as we do; it is delicious. We serve it with Basque Fries (page 198) and steamed baby carrots.

If you can't buy rabbit locally, you can order it from D'Artagnan, a New Jersey company that ships specialty meats all over the country. Call 800-DARTAG-NAN or 973-344-0565.

About 3 tablespoons unbleached all-purpose flour
One 2½- to 3-pound rabbit, cut into small pieces
Salt and fresh-ground black pepper
½ cup olive oil
4 medium carrots, chopped
2 medium onions, chopped
1 garlic clove, chopped
1 cup red Rioja wine
1 cup water
8 whole baby carrots, with leaves still attached, if they're fresh
Chopped flat-leaf parsley

1. Spread the flour in a shallow dish. Season the rabbit with salt and pepper, and dredge it in the flour. Shake off the excess flour.
2. In a large skillet or saucepan, heat the oil over high heat. Add the rabbit, and cook it for 5 to 6 minutes, turning, until it is lightly browned. Lift the meat from the pan, and set it aside.

3. Add the carrots, onions, and garlic, and cook them over medium-high heat for about 5 minutes, until the onions are lightly browned. Reduce the heat, and cook the vegetables over low heat for about 10 minutes, stirring occasionally. Add the rabbit, wine, and water, and cover the pan. Cook over low heat for about 20 minutes, until the rabbit is cooked through.

4. Steam the baby carrots for 8 to 10 minutes, until they're just tender.

5. Meanwhile, using a slotted spoon or spatula, remove the rabbit from the pan, and set it aside. Purée the remaining ingredients in the pan in a food mill, food processor, or blender. Return the sauce to the pan, add the rabbit, and heat gently. Serve the rabbit and sauce immediately, garnished with parsley and the steamed carrots.

Roasted Fresh Ham

◆ PIERNA DE CERDO ASADA ◆

Serves 8

When I bake a fresh ham, I start with a very hot oven, and then I wait for half an hour before lowering the oven heat. The high heat seals the exterior of the meat and holds in the juices. I also keep the meat moist by adding diluted wine to the pan during the baking. This traditional dish is ideal for large family gatherings, since it is easy to cook ahead of time. Serve the ham with Potato Purée (page 200) and Apple Purée (page 201).

One 8-pound fresh ham, skinned (see Notes) but not boned
2 tablespoons olive oil
Salt and fresh-ground black pepper
1 cup muscatel, port, madeira, or other sweet wine
1 cup water

continued

1. Preheat the oven to 400°F. Rub the ham with olive oil, salt, and pepper, and set it on the rack of a roasting pan. Position the pan on the center oven rack, and bake the ham for about 15 minutes. Turn the ham over, and bake it about 15 minutes more, until the meat is golden.
2. In a small pitcher or bowl, mix the wine and water.
3. Lower the oven temperature to 300°F. Add the wine and water mixture to the pan, and bake the meat for 4 hours longer, or 30 minutes per pound in addition to the initial 30 minutes. Every half hour, turn the ham and baste it with the pan drippings.
4. Lift the ham from the roasting pan, and set it aside. Pour the pan juices into a saucepan, and heat them, stirring to blend them.
5. Carve the ham, and serve it with the sauce passed separately.

NOTES: *When you buy a fresh ham leg, ask the butcher to skin it. If you must skin it yourself, use a sharp knife.*

For a thicker sauce, stir 1 teaspoon cornstarch with 2 tablespoons cold water. Stir this mixture into the sauce while heating it in the saucepan.

Marinated Pork Loin with Roasted Red Peppers

❖ CINTA DE CERDO ADOBADA CON PIMIENTOS ❖

Serves 4 to 6

In Bilbao—and indeed throughout the Basque Country—pork loin is often sold already rubbed with a red, paste-like marinade. My mother never marinated her own pork loin; instead, like every other cook in the city, she bought the pork from the butcher already marinated. She then sliced and pan-fried it for us. When I arrived in New York, I could not find pork prepared this way and so set about discovering what was in the marinade. After some trial and error, I arrived at the right proportions of garlic, oil, and paprika—and was excited at the result. This dish tastes like home to me.

Because pork loin is rarely sold in pieces as small as 2 pounds, make this dish with meat left over from Top Loin of Pork Cooked with Milk (page 115) or any other pork loin dish.

FOR THE MARINADE:

1 garlic clove

Salt

½ cup plus 2 tablespoons olive oil

2 tablespoons paprika

FOR THE PORK:

2 pounds boneless pork loin, trimmed of fat

3 tablespoons olive oil, plus more as needed

. . .

4 roasted red bell peppers (page 70), sliced

1. To prepare the marinade, mash the garlic in a mortar with a little salt. Add the olive oil and paprika, and mix until the paste is intensely red.
2. Rub the loin with the paste, and then seal the loin in plastic wrap or a plastic bag. Refrigerate the meat for 2 to 4 days.
3. To cook the pork, remove the loin from the plastic bag, and slice it crosswise ½ inch thick.
4. In a large skillet, heat the oil over high heat. Add as many pork slices as will fit in the pan without crowding, and sear them for 2 to 3 minutes. Reduce the heat, turn the pork slices, and cook them for about 3 minutes longer on each side, until the meat is cooked through. Remove the cooked slices from the pan, and cook the remaining slices in the same way, adding more oil if necessary. Serve the meat with sliced roasted red peppers.

NOTE: *When marinating the meat, store it in the coolest part of the refrigerator. In most home refrigerators, this is generally the back of the lowest shelf.*

❦ *I know of nothing* that resembles Basque *sidrerías*. If you happen to visit my homeland, do not pass up any opportunity to visit one of these informal and lovely cider houses, where a simple but tasty meal can be had for a fixed price of about 25 dollars. My favorite *sidrería*, named Zapiain, is one of the oldest, and it is only a few miles away from San Sebastián (Donostia).

Sidrerías are rustic warehouses where natural cider is stored in huge barrels, called *kupelas*. In the front section of each warehouse are over-sized charcoal-fired grills and long communal tables where guests stand to eat the limited fare. In fact, the menu of all *sidrerías* is the same—salt-cod omelet, salt cod with peppers, gigantic T-bone steaks to share, and, for dessert, quince jam and walnuts.

The fun begins when a guest decides to call out the word "*Mojón!*" At the call, thirsty guests surge toward the cider barrels, glasses in hand. The barrel tenders remove the small wooden plugs called *txotx* from the *kupelas*, and guests line up to shove their glasses under the stream, called *txiri*, of lightly fermented cider. Afterwards, it's back to the T-bones and omelets until the next customer cries out, "*Mojón!*" and the rush to the barrels is on again. Needless to say, this is a lusty and boisterous dining experience—and one that typifies the Basques' appreciation of lively good times and well-prepared, simple food and drink.

Top Loin of Pork Cooked with Milk

❖ LOMO DE CERDO EN LECHE ❖

Serves 6

When I was a child, we spent the summers at the shore in a town called Mundaka. Every morning, a nearby dairy farm delivered jugs of fresh milk to us; my mouth still waters when I remember the lovely, thick cream that rose to the top. Because the milk was delivered daily, my mother sometimes had an excess, and since she believed strongly in using every last drop or crumb of edible food, she frequently cooked this pork dish. Although we children called it "not-again pork," today I love this dish and highly recommend it. The pork cooked in milk is lovely and tender, and the pan sauce is delicious.

3 pounds boneless top loin of pork roast (see Note)
Salt and fresh-ground black pepper
1 tablespoon pork lard (optional)
1/4 cup (or, if you're omitting the lard, 1/2 cup) olive oil
3 medium onions, chopped
3 cups whole milk

1. Rub the pork loin with salt and pepper. Tie the loin with kitchen twine so that it will hold its shape during cooking (or ask the butcher to tie the loin for you).

2. In a Dutch oven or heavy stockpot, heat the lard and the olive oil (or, if you prefer, olive oil only) over medium heat. Add the onions, and sauté them for 5 to 10 minutes, until they soften and begin to brown.

3. Put the pork into the pot, and raise the heat to medium-high. Cook the pork, turning it several times, for about 10 minutes, until it is lightly browned on all sides.

4. Reduce the heat to medium, add the milk, and cover the pot. Cook the pork for about 1 hour, until the meat is cooked through.

5. Spoon the remaining contents of the pot into a blender or food processor,

continued

and purée them. Heat the sauce gently in a saucepan, if necessary, then pour it into a pitcher.

6. Cut the twine from the pork, and slice it. Serve it with the sauce passed separately.

NOTE: *Pork loin is often sold as roasts larger than 3 pounds. If you buy a larger piece of loin, cut off the excess meat (or ask the butcher to do so), and serve it as 1-inch-thick fillets or medallions. Or follow the recipe for Marinated Pork Loin with Roasted Red Peppers (page 112).*

Baked Pork Chops and Vegetables
❖ CHULETAS DE CERDO ❖

Serves 6

This is a very simple and fuss-free way to cook pork chops. It's common practice in the Basque Country to slow-cook meat in casseroles—usually made of clay—but in this recipe I first cook the chops on top of the stove and then finish them in the oven. This method keeps them moist. I like to serve these chops with Potato Purée (page 200) or with Basque Fries (page 198).

1 tablespoon pork lard (optional)
¼ cup (or, if you're omitting the lard, ½ cup) olive oil
12 thin pork chops (about 2 pounds)
3 medium tomatoes, chopped
1 medium onion, chopped
1 green bell pepper, chopped
Salt
About 1½ teaspoons sugar
2 tablespoons minced flat-leaf parsley

1. Preheat the oven to 400°F.
2. In a large, deep skillet or a pot, heat the lard and olive oil (or, if you prefer, olive oil only) over medium-high heat. Add a few chops to the pan, and cook them for about 1 minute on each side, until they are lightly browned. Using tongs or a slotted spoon, transfer the chops to a large casserole, and brown the remaining chops in the same way. Put all the chops into the casserole.
3. Reduce the heat to medium-low, and add the tomatoes, onion, and pepper to the oil in the skillet or pot. Cook the vegetables very slowly for about 30 minutes, until they are soft. Season them to taste with salt and sugar, and cook them for about 5 minutes longer, until the flavors blend.
4. Transfer the vegetables to a food mill, and purée them (if you do not have a food mill, leave the vegetables whole). Spoon the sauce over the pork chops, and bake them, uncovered, for about 15 minutes, until the chops are cooked through. Serve them garnished with parsley.

NOTE: *You can cook thin pork medallions this way, too. If you have leftover pork loin, cut it into medallions, and cook them in place of the pork chops.*

Roast Suckling Pig
✦ COCHINILLO ASADO ✦

Serves 8

Roast suckling pig is much loved in the Basque Country, although this dish is perhaps more associated with Castile. In the United States, it is difficult to find a very small pig; more easy to obtain are 20- to 25-pound pigs, destined for outdoor pig roasts. But a good butcher should be able to obtain a pig small enough to be roasted in the oven, or you can order one from D'Artagnan (800-DARTAGNAN or 973-344-0565). And it's worth the trouble! The little pigs are

continued

easy to prepare and so tender that they practically fall apart when cooked, yielding succulent, delicious meat. At home, we serve this dish with nothing more than a simple green salad.

One 6- to 7-pound suckling pig, dressed (see Note)
Salt
2 tablespoons pork lard or olive oil
1 small onion, quartered
1 garlic clove, sliced
3 or 4 sprigs flat-leaf parsley
2 cups water
½ cup dry white wine

1. Preheat the oven to 400°F.
2. Place the pig, belly-side up, in a large roasting pan. Rub the pig with salt and lard or olive oil, and scatter the onion, garlic, and parsley over. Add the water to the pan. Roast the pig for 1 hour.
3. Turn the pig skin-side up, add the wine, and baste the pig with the pan juices. Raise the heat to 500°F, and roast the pig for about 1 hour longer, until the skin is golden brown and crisp and a thermometer inserted in the thigh registers 160°F.
4. Cut the pig into pieces. Strain the pan juices, and then heat them gently. Spoon the juices over the pig, and serve.

NOTE: *Ask the butcher to split the pig's chest as well as the belly. This is a traditional way to dress suckling pig, and he should be able to do it easily (be sure he does not cut the pig's back, though). Or you can cut through the rib cage yourself.*

In the Basque Country, folk dances are defined according to function and character. At playful social celebrations a large group of men and women will dance in a circle, holding hands or handkerchiefs. In the middle of the circle, the most skilled dancer performs difficult and spectacular steps. The *aurresku* is the most famous of these circle dances.

Other dances include the *ezpatadantza* a "combat dance," in which two rival parties perform bearing swords, sticks, or wooden arches. Also popular are "witch dances," such as the *sorgin dantza*, usually performed in the village of Lasarte on carnival Sunday. Witch dances date back to ancient times, and their meanings are mostly long lost. But all these folk dances are brought to life at festive occasions by the hundreds of dance groups spread across all parts of the Basque Country.

Grilled Lamb Chops

❖ CHULETITAS DE CORDERO ❖

Serves 4

At the restaurant I grill lamb chops over charcoal or lava rocks, but at home I cook them in a skillet with very little oil, as described here. If you prefer, grill your chops. Either way, they are excellent. Serve them with Basque Fries (page 198) or Home-Style Roasted Potatoes (page 197).

¼ cup olive oil
3 garlic cloves, minced
2 tablespoons chopped flat-leaf parsley
12 small loin lamb chops (2 to 3 ounces each)
Salt

continued

1. In a bowl, mix 3 tablespoons of the oil with the garlic and the parsley. Sprinkle the chops lightly with salt, and then rub them on both sides with the garlic-parsley mixture.
2. In a large skillet, heat the remaining 1 tablespoon oil over high heat. Add the chops, and cook them for about 1 minute on each side for rare meat. For better-done meat, reduce the heat to medium, and cook the chops for 2 to 3 minutes longer on each side. Serve immediately.

Roasted Leg of Lamb

◆ PIERNA DE CORDERO BASCARAN ◆

Serves 4

My good friend José Bascaran, who raises sheep in upstate New York, supplies me with all of my lamb for the restaurants, and I am never disappointed with the quality. On the contrary—it is extraordinary. Perhaps this is because he takes such good care of his flock; he even plays soft music in the barn at night to help the sheep sleep (I would not believe this if I had not witnessed it with my own eyes and ears). José is a retired jai-alai player who competed in Florida and Connecticut before settling in New York State. His family still raises sheep and cattle in Markina in the Basque Country, and he follows the farming practices that he learned while growing up there.

One 4-pound leg of lamb
Salt
3 garlic cloves, halved
2 tablespoons pork lard
1 cup water

1. Preheat the oven to 300°F. Set an oven-proof pan or bowl on the lower rack of the oven, and fill it with water (see Note).
2. Sprinkle the lamb lightly with salt, and then rub it with the garlic halves. Rub it next with the lard, and then place it in a roasting pan.
3. Roast the leg on the center rack of the oven for 45 minutes. Turn the leg over, baste it with the pan juices, and sprinkle it with the 1 cup water. Roast the leg for 45 minutes longer, basting several times.
4. Raise the oven temperature to 450°F and roast the lamb for about 15 minutes longer, until the meat is nicely browned and forms a crunchy crust. Let it rest for a while before carving it.

NOTE: *Keeping a pan or bowl of water in the oven during roasting keeps the interior of the oven moist, which in turn keeps the meat moist.*

Baby Lamb in Rosemary Sauce

✦ CORDERITO ASADO AL ROMERO ✦

Serves 6

Baby lamb is a traditional springtime treat in the Basque Country, and in my restaurant I serve it year round; a Basque farmer in upstate New York sends me baby lambs monthly. If you can find baby lamb in a butcher's shop, try it. Never older than a month, it will have been fed exclusively with ewe's milk, making the meat tender, mild, and delicious. If baby lamb isn't available where you live, you can substitute a leg of more mature lamb.

FOR THE LAMB:
½ baby lamb, or 1 4- to 6-pound leg of lamb, fat trimmed
Salt
1 tablespoon crushed fresh rosemary
3 tablespoons olive oil

continued

1 cup water
$^{1}/_{2}$ cup plus 2 tablespoons red wine vinegar
2 tablespoons crushed fresh rosemary
1 tablespoon olive oil
1 teaspoon cornstarch

1. Preheat the oven to 450°F.
2. To prepare the lamb, rub it with the salt, rosemary, and olive oil. Put it into a shallow roasting pan, sprinkle it with a little water, and place the pan in the oven. Put a small oven-proof bowl or pan filled with water on the lowest rack of the oven, and leave it there while the meat roasts. Roast the meat for 1 hour. Turn the lamb over, and roast it for about 30 minutes to 1 hour longer, until it is done to your taste. While the lamb roasts, sprinkle it with water every 10 minutes or so.
3. Let the lamb stand for about 10 minutes after removing it from the oven. Collect the pan juices to use in the sauce.
4. To prepare the sauce, combine the water, vinegar, and rosemary in a saucepan, and bring them to a boil over high heat. Reduce the heat to low, and cook the mixture for about 10 minutes, until it is slightly reduced. Strain the mixture, and return it to the pan. Add the oil, cornstarch, and pan juices, and whisk well. Bring the sauce to a boil over medium-high heat, and cook it for 2 to 3 minutes, until it has thickened.
5. Carve the lamb, and serve each portion with some of the sauce.

NOTE: *Steam from the bowl or pan of water, and the regular sprinkling, keeps the meat succulent.*

❧ *The best-known* Basque sport is jai-alai, whose name means "gay game" or "joyful game." The best jai-alai players always attract crowds of enthusiastic fans.

Jai-alai is always played in three-walled courts, called *frontons*, but the game has several forms. *Cesta-punta* is played with a curved basket of wicker woven over chestnut wood, which is grooved for catching and throwing the ball at great speeds. *Remonte* is similar to *cesta-punta* but is played with a less curved and more compact basket. *Pala* is played with a short paddle and a heavier ball.

Cesta-punta is the only form of jai-alai that has taken hold in other parts of the world. My grandfather Claudio was one of the best *cesta-punta* players of his day; he was asked to play at the inauguration of Havana's *fronton* in 1920. He also played in the Philippines, Alexandria, Milan, Mexico, and Buenos Aires, to name only a few of the places where jai-alai became popular. Today in the United States, jai-alai is played in *frontons* in Nevada, Connecticut, and Florida.

Other Basque games are tests of endurance and strength. For example, *estropadaks* are small rowing boats with fixed seats that we use for racing. The best-known of the competitive *estropadak* regattas is held on the first Sunday of September, when thousands of fans gather in San Sebastián to watch and cheer. *Aizkoloriak* is a competition for brawny men who race the clock as they split huge tree logs with axes. *Harrija-sotzaileak* is another competition of brute strength, where men lift stones of different shapes and sizes, some of which can weigh as much as 300 kilograms (660 pounds).

Common to all sports and games is betting, a favorite spectator sport on the streets in the Basque Country.

Baby Lamb or Calf Liver with Onions

✦ HIGADITO DE CORDERO ENCEBOLLADO ✦

Serves 4

When I buy baby lambs from José Bascaran (see page 120), I look forward to preparing the tender livers as much as I do the sweet-tasting meat. If you cannot find such young lamb livers, use calf liver instead. Avoid beef or pork liver—they are far too strong-tasting. I recommend serving small portions of liver, since it is very rich. But, by all means, indulge when you can! I like to serve this dish with Home-Style Roasted Potatoes (page 197) or other simple roasted potatoes.

¹/₄ cup plus 1 tablespoon olive oil
1 pound baby lamb or calf liver, cut into narrow strips or fillets
Salt
3 medium onions, cut into strips
¹/₂ cup dry white wine
2 tablespoons chopped flat-leaf parsley

1. In a skillet, heat the olive oil over medium heat until it is very hot. Sprinkle the liver with salt, add the liver to the skillet, and fry the liver for about 2 minutes on each side, until it is lightly browned. Remove it from the pan, and set it aside.

2. Add the onion to the skillet, and cook it over medium heat, stirring often, for about 30 minutes, until the onion is very soft. Add the wine, return the liver to the pan, and cook it for about 5 minutes, until it is cooked through. Serve it garnished with parsley.

Piquillo Peppers Stuffed with Ground Meat

♦ PIMIENTOS DEL PIQUILLO RELLENOS DE CARNE ♦

Serves 4

Piquillo peppers, canned in Navarra, are available in many specialty-foods stores in the United States, and you can order them from Northern Boulevard (718-779-4971). But you can also substitute roasted whole green or red bell peppers for this very special stuffed pepper dish. In fact, my mother always used bell peppers when I was growing up, because piquillo peppers were rarely available then even in the Basque Country. When they became easier to find, however, she switched to them because of their outstanding flavor—and also, I imagine, because they came already roasted and peeled. If you decide to use bell peppers, choose small ones and serve only two per person, instead of four of the smaller piquillos.

One 2-ounce white dinner roll, kaiser roll, or other soft roll, or
2 baguette slices, torn or chopped into small pieces
$1/2$ cup white wine
5 ounces ground pork
5 ounces ground beef
Salt
$1/2$ cup plus 2 tablespoons olive oil
1 onion, minced
1 garlic clove, minced
1 tablespoon chopped flat-leaf parsley
16 canned piquillo peppers or 8 roasted, peeled, and
seeded red or green bell peppers (see page 70)
3 tablespoons unbleached all-purpose flour
2 eggs, beaten
2 cups Spanish Sauce (page 185)

continued

1. Preheat the oven to 350°F.

2. In a small bowl, combine the bread pieces and wine, and set the bowl aside.

3. In a larger bowl, combine the pork and beef. Salt the meat lightly, mix it well, and set the bowl aside.

4. In a skillet, heat ¼ cup of the oil over medium heat. Add the onion and garlic, and sauté them for about 5 minutes, until they are softened. Add the ground meat, and cook, stirring, until the onion and garlic are incorporated and the meat begins to brown. Add the parsley, bread pieces, and any wine not absorbed by the bread, and mix well. Cook the mixture for about 5 minutes, then remove the pan from the heat. Let the mixture cool slightly.

5. With a small spoon, carefully stuff each pepper with some of the meat, taking care not to tear the pepper. Close the top of the pepper with crossed toothpicks.

6. Spread the flour in a shallow dish. Put the eggs into a separate shallow dish. Lay the peppers in the flour, and turn them to coat them completely. Then put them into the egg, and turn them to coat them.

7. In a clean skillet, heat the remaining 6 tablespoons oil over medium heat. Cook the peppers in batches for about 2 minutes on each side, just until they are lightly browned. Drain them on two layers of paper towels.

8. Arrange the peppers in a shallow casserole just large enough to hold them upright without crowding. Spoon the sauce over them, and bake them, uncovered, for about 15 minutes, until the meat is hot. Serve immediately.

Veal Kidneys with Sherry Sauce

❖ RIÑONES DE TERNERA AL JEREZ ❖

Serves 6

It's a shame that Americans don't eat as much organ meat as Basques do. When well prepared, kidneys and other organ meats are excellent. Serve these with steamed white rice or with Basque Fries (page 198).

2 pounds veal kidneys, halved and trimmed of fat
Coarse salt
1/4 cup olive oil
1 medium onion, chopped
1 garlic clove, chopped
2 tablespoons chopped flat-leaf parsley
1/2 cup sherry

1. Cut the kidney halves in half again crosswise. Remove any remaining fat and gristle. Put the kidneys into a colander, and sprinkle them well with salt. Set the colander on a plate, and refrigerate the kidneys for about 1 hour. Then rinse the kidneys well under cold running water to remove the salt. Drain them.

2. In a large skillet, heat the oil over medium heat. Add the onion, and sauté it for about 5 minutes, until it is softened. Add the kidneys, reduce the heat to low, and cover the pan. Cook the kidneys for about 30 minutes, until they are tender.

3. In a mortar, mash the garlic with the parsley to form a paste. Add the sherry, and stir. Add this mixture to the skillet, and cook the kidneys for about 5 minutes longer, until the flavors are well blended. Serve immediately.

Chicken Basque-Style

✦ POLLO A LA VASCA ✦

Serves 4

We Basques rarely serve this dish with any accompaniment, but it would be very good indeed with white rice or boiled potatoes sprinkled with parsley. To reduce the cooking time, substitute four boned and skinned chicken breasts for the whole chicken, and cut the cooking time to approximately 30 minutes.

One 3- to 3½-pound chicken, cut into pieces
Coarse salt
¾ cup olive oil
3 garlic cloves, minced
1 medium onion, cut into strips
2 red bell peppers, cut into strips
2 medium tomatoes, peeled, seeded, and diced
Salt
1½ teaspoons sugar
1 cup dry white wine
Juice of ½ lemon
2 tablespoons chopped flat-leaf parsley

1. Sprinkle the chicken generously with salt. Keep the chicken in the refrigerator or another cool place while you cook the vegetables.

2. In a skillet, heat 6 tablespoons of the olive oil over medium heat. Cook the garlic for 1 to 2 minutes, until it turns golden brown. Add the onion, and sauté it for about 10 minutes, until it is softened. Add the red peppers and tomatoes, mix well, and season with salt and sugar. Cook, stirring, for about 15 minutes, until the tomatoes release their liquid.

3. In a deep skillet or stockpot, heat the remaining 6 tablespoons olive oil over high heat. Add the chicken, and cook it for 10 to 15 minutes, turning it, until it is lightly browned on all sides. Add the pepper-tomato mixture and the wine, and mix well. Reduce the heat to medium, partially cover the pot, and cook for about 40 minutes, until the sauce thickens and the chicken is cooked through.

4. Gently stir in the lemon juice, and cook 5 minutes more. Serve the chicken and sauce garnished with parsley.

Chicken Breasts with Garlic and Parsley

❖ PECHUGAS DE POLLO AL AJILLO ❖

Serves 4

For this recipe, you will need boned, skinned chicken breasts. Because the breasts are to be sliced horizontally, not cut in half vertically, be sure they are whole when you buy them. If you cannot buy whole boned breasts, buy bone-in breasts or whole chickens, and cut the meat from the bone yourself. These breasts are seasoned with a typical Basque mixture of parsley, garlic, and olive oil.

2 whole boned, skinned chicken breasts
Salt
4 garlic cloves, minced
2 tablespoons chopped flat-leaf parsley
About 6 tablespoons olive oil

continued

1. Using a sharp boning or slicing knife, cut the chicken breasts in half horizontally to make four pieces, each of them half the thickness of a whole breast. Lightly sprinkle the pieces with salt, and set them aside on a dish.

2. In a small bowl, mix the garlic, parsley, and 3 tablespoons of the olive oil. Rub the mixture on both sides of the chicken pieces.

3. In a large skillet, heat about 1½ tablespoons of the olive oil over high heat. Add as many of the chicken pieces as will fit in the pan without crowding, and cook them for about 1 minute. Reduce the heat to medium, and cook the chicken pieces for about 2 minutes. Turn them over, raise the heat to high, and cook them for 1 minute. Reduce the heat to medium again, and cook the chicken for about 2 minutes longer, or until it is cooked through. Remove the chicken from the pan, and keep it warm. Cook the remaining pieces the same way, adding more oil to the pan as needed. Serve the chicken immediately.

HAPPY HENS

❧ *I am pleased* to see that eggs are regaining their good reputation. The scientific community has rethought its position on the dangers of the cholesterol in egg yolks, so most people no longer need to worry about eating a few eggs a week. When I read an article by Molly O'Neill in the *New York Times* (September 1997) decreeing that eggs were no longer "in the dog house," my reaction was "Hooray!"

In the Basque Country, we can still get our eggs from what I call "happy hens"—birds that are able to wander freely around farmyards. In the United States, these are called free-range chickens, which I think is a rather boring name. Whatever you call them, though, happy hens lay delicious eggs, and their meat is superior, too.

It is common in the Basque Country, as you will see from reading these recipes, to add scrambled or poached eggs to some first courses to convert them into light meals.

Roasted Chicken

❖ POLLO ASADO ❖

Serves 4

Ilearned to roast chicken in this simple yet delicious method from a dear friend who otherwise could not cook at all. She was our neighbor during summers in Mundaka, and we children always turned up at her door when she roasted a plump chicken. Over the years, everyone who has tried this recipe has been very pleased with it. I always try to cook with free-range, farm-raised chickens—which I call happy hens. They are more expensive than other fowl, but their flavor is far superior. I love this dish preceded by a green salad and served with Basque Fries (page 198). My youngest sons, Alex and Lucas, say this is "the best chicken in the world."

One 3- to 4-pound chicken
Salt
2 beef bouillon cubes
1 lemon
1 tablespoon lard or olive oil
$\frac{1}{2}$ cup beer (optional)
$\frac{1}{4}$ cup water

1. Preheat the oven to 350°F. Sprinkle the chicken with salt inside and out. Insert one bouillon cube into the chicken's cavity. Using a sharp knife, trim off the ends of the lemon, and make a few deep incisions in the lemon. Put the lemon into the breast cavity, and then insert the other bouillon cube.
2. Rub the chicken with lard or oil, and set it, breast up, in a roasting pan. Roast the chicken for 8 minutes, then turn it breast down and baste it. After 8 minutes more, turn it breast-side up and baste it again. Continue turning and basting the chicken about every 8 minutes until it has roasted for 1 hour.
3. After 1 hour, increase the oven temperature to 450°F, and add the beer, if you're using it. Roast the chicken 15 minutes more, until it is crisp and golden.

continued

4. Lift the chicken from the pan, and set it on a platter. Put the pan on a burner, and add the water. Cook the juices over high heat, stirring, until they are boiling and blended. Serve the pan juices with the carved chicken.

NOTE: *The beer adds another flavor dimension to the chicken, but it is not necessary. Try the chicken both ways. Use dark or light beer, frothy or flat.*

Stuffed Christmas Capon

❖ CAPÓN RELLENO DE NAVIDAD ❖

Serves 8

Capons, 10- to 12-month-old castrated chickens, are plump and tender birds that have long been traditional Christmastime fare in the Basque Country. In Bilbao, December 21 is the day of the spectacular Santo Tomás Fair, where local farmers sell capons and late-fall produce to bustling shoppers anxious to buy the food for their Christmas feasts. I try not to miss the fair—it's so much a part of the holiday season for me.

I have noticed capons in more American markets recently than when I first arrived here, perhaps because of an increased interest in free-range poultry. But if you can't find capon locally, you can order it from D'Artagnan (800-DARTAGNAN or 973-344-0565).

One 5- to 6-pound capon or large roasting hen
Salt
¼ cup olive oil
4 firm, tart apples, such as Granny Smith or Fuji, peeled, cored, and cut into 6 wedges each
10 dates
1 cup dry white wine
2 cups homemade (page 194) or commercial chicken broth

1. Preheat the oven to 400°F.

2. Lightly sprinkle the chicken inside and out with salt. Rub it inside and out with a little of the olive oil.

3. Insert the apple wedges and dates into the breast cavity, and put the chicken breast-up in a shallow roasting pan. Place the pan on the center rack of the oven, reduce the heat to 300°F, and roast the chicken for 1½ hours (15 minutes to the pound). Baste the chicken with the pan juices every 10 to 15 minutes. During the final 10 minutes of roasting, raise the oven temperature to 450°F to brown the chicken nicely.

4. Lift the chicken from the pan, and set it on a platter. Remove the apples and dates from the cavity, and put them into a small bowl. Cover the chicken to keep it warm. Using a fork, mash the apples and dates until the mixture is quite smooth.

5. Pour the contents of the pan into a saucepan, add the wine and broth, and bring the liquid to a boil over high heat. Boil it for about 10 minutes, until it is reduced by half. Serve the sauce and mashed fruit with the capon.

CHRISTMAS CAPON, COOKED IN THE OLD STYLE

❦ *José Garzón Saez* writes about Basque Christmas traditions in his book *Platos de Navidad*. Before Basque housewives, or *etxekoandres*, had ovens in their homes, writes Saez, when it came time to cook the Christmas capon these ingenious cooks would cross two wooden spoons near the bottom of a large, deep clay pot, and set the plump bird on them. The spoons held the capon above the fat in the bottom of the pot. The *etxekoandres* would then cover the pot and cook the capon over medium heat for about three hours. And, without exception, the women rubbed the bird with lard, never olive oil. Some Basques still say that capon tastes best when cooked this way.

Quails in Chocolate Sauce

Serves 4

My older brother Valeriano is an avid hunter and fisherman. During our summer vacations by the sea in Mundaka, he spent all day fishing with his harpoon, but as soon as autumn arrived he hunted upland game nearly every weekend. When he came home with quails, my mother frequently prepared them as I describe here. The bit of chocolate ("a piece about the size of a chestnut," my mother explained) adds richness to the sauce for the little birds.

8 quails (see Notes)
Salt
1 cup plus about 2 tablespoons olive oil
4 medium onions, chopped
8 medium carrots, sliced thin
6 garlic cloves, sliced
2 tablespoons chopped flat-leaf parsley
8 black peppercorns
½ cup plus 2 tablespoons dry white wine
½ cup plus 2 tablespoons red wine vinegar
16 pearl onions (optional)
2 ounces unsweetened chocolate, coarsely chopped
4 slices white bread

1. Sprinkle the quails with the salt, and, if the butcher hasn't done so, truss them. Do this by folding the legs and tying them against the body with cotton string.

2. In a large pot, heat 1 cup of olive oil over medium heat. Add the onions, carrots, garlic, parsley, and peppercorns. Raise the heat to high, and cook the vegetables, stirring with a wooden spoon, for about 10 minutes, until the onions begin to brown.

3. Add the quails, and cook them for 3 to 4 minutes on each side, until they are lightly browned.

4. Add the wine and vinegar, and cover the pan. Cook the quails over medium-low heat for about 30 minutes, or until the juices run clear when the quails are pricked in the thigh with a small sharp knife or a fork. With a slotted spoon, transfer the quails to a platter. Cover them, and keep them warm.

5. Meanwhile, bring a saucepan of water to a boil over high heat, and add the pearl onions, if you are using them. Reduce the heat, and simmer the onions for about 20 minutes, until they are tender. Drain them, and set them aside.

6. Stir the liquid in the pan in which the quails were cooked, and add a little water if the liquid is too thick. Add the chocolate, and stir until it is melted and blended with the pan juices. Add the pearl onions, if you are using them, and stir gently. Return the quails to the pan, and, continuously spooning the sauce over them, cook them over low heat for about 10 minutes, until the sauce is thick and coats the quails.

7. Meanwhile, in a skillet, heat the remaining 2 tablespoons of oil over medium-high heat. Lay the bread in the oil, and fry the bread for about 1 minute on each side, until it is lightly browned.

8. Untruss the quails. Lay the bread on serving plates, and top each slice with two quails. Spoon the sauce over the quails, and garnish each serving with four pearl onions, if you like.

NOTES: *Ask the butcher to truss the little birds for you. If you prefer, you can use boned quail, which is easier to eat than bone-in quail and available in some specialty-foods stores. The cooking time is the same.*

   If you can't get quail locally, you can order it from D'Artagnan (800-DARTAGNAN or 973-344-0565).

Roasted Duck

◆ PATO ASADO ◆

Serves 4

Duck has figured in numerous culinary traditions for centuries. References to duck can be found in histories of the ancient Chinese and, on the other side of the world, the Romans. Basques, who have inhabited the same portion of the Iberian Peninsula since prehistoric times, have been eating duck since the birds first flew over our waterways. This is a simple preparation that relies on common vegetables and tart apples to enhance the natural richness of duck. Serve the duck with Potato Purée (page 200), Home-Style Roasted Potatoes (page 197), or another potato dish.

One 3- to 4-pound duck
Salt
¼ cup plus 1 tablespoon olive oil
2 medium onions, chopped
2 carrots, sliced
3 firm, tart apples, such as Granny Smith or Fuji, peeled,
cored, and cut into 6 wedges each
10 dates
1 cup white wine

1. Lightly sprinkle the duck inside and out with salt. Using a small, sharp knife, make several slits in the skin to release fat during roasting.

2. In a flame-proof casserole, heat the oil over high heat. Add the duck, and cook it for about 15 minutes, turning it several times, until it is golden on all sides.

3. Reduce the heat to medium, add the onions and carrots, and cover the casserole. Cook the vegetables for about 15 minutes, until the onions soften. Add the apples and dates, and mix well. Continue cooking, covered, over medium-low heat for about 15 minutes, until the apples and carrots

start to soften. Add the wine, cover the casserole, and cook for about 30 minutes, stirring occasionally to prevent burning.

4. Lift the duck from the casserole, and carve it. Heat the remaining contents of the pan, and serve them as a sauce with the duck.

NOTE: *If you prefer, purée the vegetables and liquid in a blender, food processor, or food mill before heating them gently to serve with the duck.*

Country-Style Pheasant

❖ FAISÁN DE CAMPO ❖

Serves 6

Pheasant is a full-flavored bird that is most often considered to be wild game. However, many butchers and specialty markets sell farm-raised birds, particularly in the fall of the year, as does D'Artagnan, a New Jersey company that ships specialty meats all over the United States (call 800-DARTAGNAN or 973-344-0565). My brothers were avid hunters, so when I was growing up we often had fresh pheasant, and I am extremely fond of it. But even if you know no hunters, I hope you will try this lovely dish.

Two 2- to 3-pound pheasants
Salt and fresh-ground white pepper
3 tablespoons lard or olive oil
4 bacon slices
2 large onions, chopped
2 carrots, sliced
1 bunch mixed fresh herbs, such as thyme and flat-leaf parsley,
tied with kitchen twine

continued

1 quart homemade (page 195) or commercial beef broth
1 cup dry white wine
2 tablespoons unsalted butter, melted (optional)
1 tablespoon unbleached all-purpose flour (optional)

1. Lightly sprinkle the pheasants inside and out with salt and pepper. Rub the outside of each pheasant with about 1 tablespoon lard or olive oil, and lay two slices of bacon over each pheasant. Truss the pheasants with kitchen twine, tying the legs, wings, and bacon against each body.

2. In a large pot, heat the remaining lard or olive oil over high heat. Add the pheasants, and cook them for about 15 minutes, turning them several times, until they are golden on all sides.

3. Reduce the heat to medium. Add the onions, carrots, and herbs, cover the pot, and cook for about 15 minutes, until the onions soften.

4. Raise the heat to high. Add the broth and white wine, and bring them to a boil. Reduce the heat to medium, and cook the pheasants, covered, for about 45 minutes, until the juices run clear when the thighs are pierced with a small sharp knife or fork.

5. Remove the herbs from the pot. Remove the birds, cut the twine, and carve the pheasants. Transfer the remaining contents of the pot to a food processor or blender, and purée them. For a thicker sauce, transfer the blended sauce to a saucepan. Whisk together the butter and flour, and add the mixture to the pan. Whisking constantly, bring the sauce to a boil, and cook it for about 5 minutes, until it is thick. Spoon the sauce over the pheasants, and serve them.

❦ *Spain is the third* largest wine-producing country in the world; only France and Italy exceed Spain's output. Spanish wines are primarily identified by their growing regions, known as *denominaciones de origen* (D.O.). There are more than fifty such denominations, some of the best-known being Rioja, Ribera del Duero, Rias Baixas, and Penedés. Rioja, the most widely recognized denomination, was also the first to be officially designated.

The Rioja region is situated to the southwest of the Pyrenees. The Sierra de Cantabria mountains are to the north and west of Rioja, and the Sierra de la Demanda to the south. Named after the Rio Oja, a tributary of the Ebro River, Rioja is divided into three areas: Rioja Alta in the western highlands, Rioja Baja in the lower plains to the south and east, and Rioja Alavesa to the northwest, in the Basque province of Alava. Rioja Alavesa, a stunningly scenic area, is home to such historic wine-making towns and villages as Elciego, Oyon, Laguardia, and Samaniego, each worth a day's visit.

Rioja wines, particularly those from Rioja Alta and Rioja Alavesa, are the most commonly consumed in the Basque Country. Generally, Basques prefer red wines to white, and they appreciate the beautifully transparent, ruby color of Rioja reds. As a rule, these wines are lighter than the deeper, more full-bodied reds from France, Italy, and California. Their characteristic transparency is a result of their high proportion of *tempranillo* grapes (*temprano* means "early," and the grape is so named because it ripens from mid-September to early October, a full two weeks before other Rioja grapes). These unique characteristics make Rioja wines a perfect match for nearly any meat, fish, or poultry dish. Lightness and transparency, however, do not diminish the complexity of our *reservas* and *gran reservas*.

White Wines: Basques may drink far more red wine than white, but we appreciate white wines, especially in the heat of summer and with certain seafood dishes. Our most distinctive white wine is made not in Rioja but in our own coastal provinces. From the white wine grapes that grow on our rugged coast, nearly to the edge of the sea, we make *txakolí*, considered almost a national drink. Light, clean-tasting, and pleasantly acidic, txakolí wines are usually unfiltered and sometimes *petillant*— slightly sparkling, but not so effervescent that they can be labeled sparkling wine. These characteristics make them perfect matches with crustaceans and other fresh seafood. Txakolí are nice summer wines, and their low alcohol content (10.5 to 11 percent) make them good with lunch or as aperitifs.

In the Basque Country, there are dozens of txakolí labels. The best known txakolí D.O., though, is Getaria, a town about 40 miles to the west of San Sebastián with no more than 85 hectares of vineyards, which makes it the smallest D.O. in Spain. Because of such limited production, these wines are consumed almost exclusively in the Basque Country, although a few find their way to other parts of Europe. Txomin Etxaniz is a txakolí that is exported to the United States through Fine Estates of Spain, a company in Dedham, Massachusetts. Because txakolí are artisanal rather than mass-produced wines, they are rather expensive.

Red Wines: Red wine is the favorite accompaniment for most Basque meals. We also drink it with *pinchos* (snacks), or by itself as a *chiquito*, or "little one"—a 3- to 4-ounce serving of wine that costs less than a dollar at most bars.

There are four categories of red wine; these are determined by the aging process, which is reflected in the quality and price level. The age of a Spanish wine is clearly noted on the small, numbered label on the back of every bottle, which declares the wine's denomination of origin and its category as (1) *sin crianza*, (2) *crianza*, (3) *reserva*, or (4) *gran reserva*.

Traditionally, *bodegas* (wineries) aged their wines for many years in 225-liter *barricas* (barrels) of American or French oak, but recently there has been a trend to age wines in both oak and the bottle to help them reach their full potential. The *sin crianza* or *vino joven* (young wine) is not aged in oak; it is comparable to the French *Beaujolais*. Wines labeled *crianza*, which means "aged in oak," require at least two years' aging, of which a minimum of one year must be in oak and the remainder in the bottle. *Reserva* wines are required to be aged in oak for a minimum of one year, followed by two years in the bottle. *Gran reservas* require at least two years in oak casks and no fewer than three years in the bottle. These official regulations do not restrict the individual *bodeguero* (wine maker) from choosing to age his wines longer.

Aging is usually done only in good and very good years for *reservas* and in very good to excellent years for *gran reservas*. Red wines are aged for longer periods than whites, although some whites, such as Rioja wines made with local viura grapes, are traditionally aged in oak barrels, too.

I have some favorite red wines from Rioja Alavesa, Rioja Alta, and even from the D.O. of Navarra, which produces exquisite wines quite similar in style to those of Rioja. All these wines are now available in the United States, and whenever I see them I feel as if I am at home in Spain. Although the vintages are recent, I recognize many of the labels from my youth and my parents' house.

I highly recommend Vina Tondonia, made by R. Lopez de Heredia, one of Rioja's oldest wineries, established in 1877. My dear American friend Gerry Dawes, who is an enthusiastic expert in Spanish wine and gastronomy, rates Viña Tondonia Reserva 1990 with 92 points (out of 100), describing it as "complex, full, mature, with a lively, firm, oaky finish." Viña Tondonia is imported to the United States by Think Global in Santa Barbara, California.

Another favorite from Rioja Alta is Bodegas Muga, a wine that ranks among the best that Rioja has to offer in terms of tradition and quality. Muga has beautiful *crianzas*, *reservas*, and *gran reservas*, the last bearing the name Prado Enea. This winery also offers a new high-end label called Torremuga; the *reserva* 1991 earned 95 points from Dawes. Muga is available in the United States through Fine Estates from Spain.

One of Rioja Alavesa's finest wineries is Granja Nuestra Señora de Remelluri. The owner's son Telmo Rodriguez, whom I know well, spent some time in nearby France, which may explain why his wines resemble French wines in style, and why his *bodega* is among very few in Rioja simply to state the harvest year on the label, and not the category (*crianza*, *reserva*, or *gran reserva*). Remelluri wines are also available through Fine Estates from Spain.

Another favorite of mine is a wine from Navarra, Gran Feudo, made by Bodegas Julian Chivite and available through CIV, U.S.A. in Sacramento, California. This beautifully soft wine is made of *tempranillo* grapes blended with small amounts of cabernet and merlot. During a recent tasting in Navarra, my friend Gerry Dawes gave the "Coleccion 125 Aniversario" a rating of 94 points.

Chivite also makes a magnificent *rosado* (rosé) that ranks among the world's best. I have found that drinking *rosado* can become a delightful habit, particularly in the summer when a glass of chilled *rosado* makes a perfect cocktail or meal accompaniment. And I love the pretty color.

There are so many more wonderful wines from Rioja and surrounding regions that I cannot mention them all. I hope you will enjoy trying them to discover your own favorites.

Fillet of Hake with Clams and Shrimp in Parsley-Garlic Sauce

❖ MERLUZA EN SALSA VERDE ❖

Serves 4

Salsa verde, or green sauce, is used frequently with various fish and vegetables. Hake is a favorite fish in the Basque Country, but this preparation is equally delicious with monkfish or any other firm-fleshed fish. My family ate this and similar dishes in the summertime, when we spent three long, happy months at the seashore. But even during the summer, my parents were strict about everyone showing up for meals on time: 8:00 A.M. for breakfast, 2:00 P.M. for lunch, and 9:30 P.M. for dinner. I remember my older brothers and sisters complaining because they would have to leave their friends in order to be punctual—but we could never miss a family meal. Since my mother was such a good cook, though, no one really minded.

continued

12 Manila clams, well scrubbed (see Note)
2 cups water
About 1 cup unbleached all-purpose flour
2 pounds hake fillet, cut into 16 pieces
Salt
½ cup olive oil
2 garlic cloves, minced
2 tablespoons dry white wine
½ cup minced flat-leaf parsley
12 medium shrimp, peeled
Chopped flat-leaf parsley, for garnish (optional)

1. In a small saucepan, combine the clams with the water, and bring them to a boil over high heat. Reduce the heat to medium-high, and cook for about 5 minutes, until the clams open. Drain the clams, reserving ½ cup of the cooking liquid. Discard any clams that do not open, and set the rest aside.

2. Spread the flour in a shallow bowl or dish. Sprinkle the fillet pieces on both sides with salt. Dredge the fillet pieces in the flour, turning them to coat all sides. Shake the excess flour from the fish pieces, and set them aside.

3. In a large skillet or sauté pan, heat the oil over medium heat. Add the garlic, and sauté it for about 1 minute, until the garlic is light golden.

4. Lay the hake in the pan in a single layer, and cook it over medium-low heat for 1 to 2 minutes per side, until it is opaque throughout.

5. Add the wine, the ½ cup minced parsley, and the reserved clam liquid, and simmer for 1 minute, gently shaking the pan to prevent sticking. Add the clams and shrimp, and simmer for 2 to 3 minutes, until the shrimp turn pink. Garnish with a little more parsley, if you like, and serve.

NOTE: *You should be able to get Manila clams from a reputable fishmonger, but you may have to special-order them. If they are not available, substitute littleneck or slightly larger cherrystone clams. Cockles are a good substitute, too, although they may be hard to find.*

Lightly Puffed Pan-Fried Hake or Scrod

◆ MERLUZA O BACALAO FRESCO REBOZADO ◆

Serves 4

I call this fish "lightly puffed" because of the way I make the egg batter. First, I beat the egg whites until they are very foamy, and then I gently whisk the egg yolks into the whites before dipping the floured fish into the eggs. This results in a light, puffed coating on the cooked fish. Throughout the Basque Country, you will find all types of filleted fish pan-fried this way. The fish is great with a green salad and Basque Fries (page 198).

2 pounds hake or scrod (young cod) fillets, cut into 1-inch-by-2-inch pieces (see Note)
3 tablespoons unbleached all-purpose flour
Salt
2 large eggs, separated
½ cup olive oil

1. Flatten the fillets with your palm to an even ³/₄-inch thickness, taking special care with the thicker ends.
2. Spread the flour in a shallow dish. Season the hake with salt, and dredge it with flour. Shake off the excess flour, and set the hake aside.
3. Using a wire whisk or a fork, beat the whites in a bowl to the "snow point"—until they are very foamy, just before they start to thicken to soft peaks. Lightly whisk the yolks, and then stir them into the beaten whites until the mixture is smooth.
4. In a large skillet, heat the oil over medium-high heat. Dip the fillet pieces into the egg, and then drop them into the pan. Reduce the heat to medium-low, and fry the fish for about 2 minutes. Raise the heat back to medium-high. After about 30 seconds, turn the fillets. Reduce the heat to medium-low again, and fry the fish 2 minutes more. Using a slotted spoon or tongs, remove the fish, and drain it on two layers of paper towels. Serve at once.

continued

NOTE: *Fresh cod tastes similar to hake, a distant cousin that swims in nearby water but is less plentiful and more expensive. When battered, both fishes look alike, which prompts the saying, "Que te conozco bacalao, aunque vengas albardao." "Cod, I recognize you, even if you come battered." We say this when someone tries to pass off a less valuable item for a more valuable one.*

THE NOBLE HAKE

❧ *Although we Basques* prepare hake just as we do scrod, hake has, I think, a subtler flavor and more delicate texture. It is also more expensive. The two fishes look similar, so you have to be diligent when ordering hake in a restaurant; be sure you are not served scrod instead. Once you have tried both, you will know the difference by taste.

One of the best places to eat hake in the Basque Country is Kirol, a tiny restaurant in Bilbao where the fish is cooked to perfection. When I go home, I never miss an opportunity to occupy one of Kirol's five tables.

At Kirol and elsewhere in the Basque Country, hake is frequently cooked in our simple green sauce (*salsa verde*). The sauce never obscures the flavor of the fish. Basque cooks relish the flavors and textures of all our sauces, but most of all, we appreciate the intrinsic flavors of the foods we're saucing.

Fresh Cod with Red and Black Sauces

✦ BACALAO FRESCO GORRI BELTZ ✦

Serves 4

Codfish is as delicious fresh as dried. In the United States, young cod, weighing less than 2 pounds or so, is often called scrod. This is what you will need for this recipe. It is typical of many in the Basque Country in that the fish is very simply cooked, and served with one or more of our traditional sauces and some roasted peppers. Nothing more—and nothing could be easier.

In Euskera, the Basque language, *gorri* means red and *beltz* means black. Here the red is Biscayne Sauce, the black Squid Ink Sauce.

1½ pounds fresh scrod (young cod) fillets, cut into 2-inch-square pieces
Salt
2 tablespoons olive oil
½ cup Biscayne Sauce, heated (page 187)
½ cup Squid Ink Sauce, heated (page 176)
1 cup chopped warm roasted red bell peppers (see page 70)

1. Preheat the oven to 450°F.
2. Lightly sprinkle the cod pieces with salt.
3. Pour the oil into a shallow casserole. Lay the cod in the casserole, and bake it for about 10 minutes, or until it is opaque throughout.
4. Spoon the Biscayne Sauce over half of each of four heated plates. Spoon the Squid Ink Sauce on the other half of each plate. Arrange two or three pieces of cod in the center of the plate to cover the line where the sauces meet. Top the cod with the peppers, and serve immediately.

Cod-Stuffed Piquillo Peppers with Biscayne Sauce

◆ PIMIENTOS DEL PIQUILLO RELLENOS DE BACALAO ◆

CON SALSA VIZCAÍNA

Serves 4

Piquillo peppers are a delicacy that we in the Basque Country indulge in whenever we can. The peppers are grown in neighboring Navarra, where the climate and soil are favorable for their cultivation. They are hand-picked, roasted in brick ovens, peeled by hand, and then packed in glass jars or cans. Look for them in specialty-foods stores. In this recipe, they are stuffed with salt cod for a typical Basque taste treat, and served with Biscayne sauce, which is made with sweet, dry choricero peppers. You can serve Spanish Sauce (page 185) in place of Biscayne Sauce, if you prefer. The salt cod must be soaked for 24 to 36 hours to reduce the saltiness, so allow yourself plenty of time.

1/2 pound skinned and boned salt cod
3 tablespoons olive oil
1 tablespoon unbleached all-purpose flour
3 cups milk, heated
12 canned piquillo peppers (see Note); canned pimientos; or roasted,
peeled, and seeded red bell peppers (see page 70)
2 cups Biscayne Sauce (page 187)

1. In a shallow bowl, cover the fish with cold water. Refrigerate the fish for 24 to 36 hours, changing the water every 8 hours or so. Drain the fish on paper towels, and shred it with your fingers.

2. In a skillet or sauté pan, heat the oil over medium heat. Add the fish, and sauté it for about 5 minutes, until it is lightly browned. Add the flour, and mix well. Cook for 15 to 20 minutes, adding the milk a little at a time and stirring until the cod béchamel is smooth. Set the pan aside, and let the béchamel cool.

3. Preheat the oven to 350°F.

4. Using a teaspoon, stuff the peppers with the béchamel. Arrange the peppers in a casserole just large enough to hold them snugly. Spoon the Biscayne Sauce over the peppers, and bake them, uncovered, for about 5 to 10 minutes, or until they are heated through and the sauce is bubbling. Serve immediately

NOTE: *Piquillo peppers are imported from Navarra and sold in cans or jars. Buy them in specialty-foods stores, or order them from Northern Boulevard (718-779-4971).*

SALT COD

❧ *In the Basque* Country, the word *bacalao* refers to salted, dried cod; when we mean fresh cod, we say, "*bacalao fresco.*" This shows in what high regard we hold the salted product, which is as delicious as it is dear to the hearts of my countrymen and -women.

Basques are widely admired for their ways with cod, both on the sea and in the kitchen. We have been fishing for cod for centuries. According to Mark Kurlansky, author of *Cod: A Biography of the Fish that Changed the World*, Basque fishermen fished the fertile cod grounds off the Atlantic coast of North America long before Columbus sailed to the New World. Few people have known about this practice because, frankly, the Basque fishermen wanted to keep the location of these fishing grounds to themselves. Because cod fishermen sailed so far from home in search of the fish, they cured much of it with salt to preserve it during the return journey. The Basques' long reliance on salted, dried cod may partly explain why we are partial to this boldly flavored dried fish despite having plenty of fresh fish in the Basque Country.

In the United States, salt cod is imported primarily from Canada and

Norway. Canadian salt cod is cured for 30 days, Norwegian salt cod for 60 days. Both are very good, but I prefer the Norwegian—it is a little stronger and more like the bacalao I ate when I was growing up. Salt cod is relatively easy to find in American fish stores, grocery stores, and supermarkets, particularly in regions with sizable Italian and Portuguese populations.

You can buy salt cod as a whole fish, or *bacalada*; in a smaller piece, with the skin and bones; or with the skin and bones removed. Regardless of the type, salt cod must be soaked to reduce its extreme saltiness. This is easily accomplished by covering the fish with cold water and then refrigerating it for 24 to 36 hours. Change the water three or four times, or about every 8 hours. Depending on the curing method, the fish may be mild enough to eat after 24 hours, or it may require the full 36 hours. Taste the fish after 24 hours; if its flavor is appealing, drain it and proceed with the recipe. The soaked fish will be thicker because of the water it has absorbed, and it will be far more flexible than the stiff, board-like specimen with which you began. To me, the transformation always seems like a small miracle!

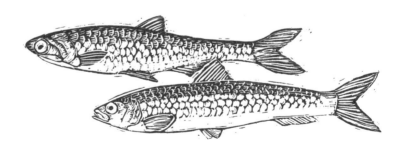

Salt Cod Pil Pil

❧ BACALAO AL PIL PIL ❧

Salt cod, or *bacalao*, is eaten throughout the Basque Country, and just about everyone there loves this ancient way of cooking it. When I serve *bacalao al pil pil* at the restaurant, it is extremely well received by my customers, too. And John Mariani, a food critic for *Esquire* and *Travel and Leisure*, came home from a visit to the Basque Country particularly impressed with this dish.

Bacalao al pil pil is technically difficult to make, but not too hard for the home cook to master. I highly recommend using a high-quality clay casserole, as we do at home. The casserole must be flame-proof and not too heavy. Many cookware stores and some large specialty-foods stores carry such casseroles, and you can also order them from Northern Boulevard (718-779-4971) in Queens, New York.

Be sure to use olive oil for the *pil pil*; another oil will not achieve the same emulsion. You'll need a full-bodied olive oil.

If you use a hot pepper, it should be only mildly hot, and flexible enough to cut into rings.

> *2 pounds salt cod, with bones and skin, cut into 3-inch-square pieces*
> *1½ to 2 cups olive oil*
> *3 garlic cloves, sliced lengthwise*
> *1 small dry hot pepper, seeded and cut into rings (optional)*

1. In a shallow bowl, cover the fish with cold water. Refrigerate the fish for 24 to 36 hours, changing the water every 8 hours or so. Drain the fish on paper or cloth towels.
2. In a large skillet, heat the olive oil over medium heat. Add the garlic and, if you like, the pepper, and cook them for 3 or 4 minutes, until the garlic is golden brown. Set the skillet aside until the garlic and pepper cool slightly.

continued

When they are cool enough to handle, remove the garlic and pepper, and reserve both for garnish. Keep the olive oil warm in the skillet.

3. Pat the salt cod dry. Using a small, sharp knife, scrape off the scales, taking care not to remove the skin. Put the fish in a separate skillet, and cover it with cold water. Bring the water to a simmer over medium heat, and cook the fish for 10 minutes, making sure that the water never boils.

   Remove the salt cod, and drain it on paper or cloth towels. Reserve ½ cup of the liquid. When the fish is cool, carefully remove the bones, taking care not to break the fish into smaller pieces. (Removing the bones is much easier after cooking than before.)

4. Lay the fish skin-side up in a 12-inch-diameter earthenware casserole. Set the casserole over low heat, and add the reserved warm olive oil 1 tablespoon at a time while shaking the casserole with a rhythmic, circular motion. Never add the next tablespoon until the one preceding it has been incorporated into the emulsion. The oil will help release the gelatin under the fish skin so that as you proceed a white sauce, resembling a light mayonnaise, will develop. The sauce will take from 15 to 30 minutes to make, depending on the quality of the cod and the olive oil. If the emulsion isn't developing, sprinkle over the sauce some of the liquid in which the cod simmered, and continue shaking the casserole.

5. To serve, put two pieces of cod on each plate, and spoon some of the sauce from the casserole over it. Garnish the plates with the reserved garlic and the hot pepper, if you've used it.

NOTE: *It's important to leave the skin on the cod when you scrape off the scales, because the skin contains a gelatinous substance that is essential to making the sauce. If you reheat this dish, begin the process in a 350°F oven, and then complete the heating on the stove, shaking the dish in the same circular motion. For a successful emulsion, be sure the olive oil is the same temperature as the fish; both should be warm.*

SALT COD CLUB RANERO–STYLE
Bacalao al Club Ranero

Around 1900, Alejandro Caveriviere, a famed French chef, moved to Bilbao, where he worked until his retirement in 1936 in several elegant, trend-setting restaurants and clubs. While working at one of these establishments, he reportedly combined two classic Basque recipes, *bacalao al pil pil* and *pisto a la bilbaína* (Vegetable Stew, page 51) to create an entirely different dish.

To make Codfish Club Ranero–Style, prepare the pil pil as described in the recipe. Add 2 cups of the pisto (made without the eggs!), and shake the casserole with a circular motion over low heat until all the ingredients are evenly mixed. Serve the dish warm. If you are using leftover pil pil, reduce the amount of pisto accordingly.

Salt Cod Biscayne-Style
❖ BACALAO A LA VIZCAÍNA ❖

Serves 4

I could not write a book about the cooking of my homeland without including this traditional Basque dish, which relies on salt cod as well as our much-loved Biscayne Sauce. Unhappily, the choricero peppers necessary for the sauce are unavailable in the United States, but you can substitute dried red peppers from California or Mexico for a good, though not quite authentic, sauce. (I have seen recipes for *bacalao a la vizcaína* in other books, in particular those on Caribbean food, but whereas these versions might be tasty, they are not authentically Basque, either.) I like this dish even more the day after it is made.

continued

2 pounds salt cod, with bones and skin, cut into 3-inch-square pieces
3 cups Biscayne Sauce (page 187)

1. In a shallow bowl, cover the fish with cold water. Refrigerate the fish for 24 to 36 hours, changing the water every 8 hours or so.
2. Transfer the cod to a large saucepan or a stockpot. Add enough cold water to cover the fish by 1 to 2 inches. Over medium heat, bring the water to a simmer; do not let it boil. Simmer the cod for about 10 minutes, until it is tender and flaky. Drain it, pat it dry, and then remove the bones without breaking the cod pieces. (Removing the bones is much easier after cooking than before.) Leave the skin on.
3. Put the cod skin-side up in a flame-proof earthenware casserole large enough to hold the pieces in a single layer. Spoon the sauce over the cod, and cook over low heat for about 15 minutes, until the fish and sauce are hot. Serve immediately.

Salt Cod Ajoarriero-Style

❖ BACALAO AJOARRIERO ❖

Serves 4

This *bacalao* dish originated in Navarra. Although today Navarra is an autonomous community of Spain, it is part of the greater Basque region called Euskal Herria. This explains why Basque and Navarran cuisines so heavily influence each other. There are numerous recipes for this dish—some have potatoes, and others include lobster and other shellfish—but I find this straightforward preparation the most true to its roots. The salt cod in this dish is shredded, so if you buy a whole *bacalada*, you can save the attractive center sections for preparations such as Salt Cod Pil Pil (page 151) or Salt Cod Biscayne-Style (page 153), and rely on the outer sections of the fish for this. *Bacalao Ajoarriero* is robust enough to need no accompaniment except bread and wine.

2 pounds boned and skinned salt cod, cut into small pieces
About 2 cups olive oil
2 garlic cloves, sliced
2 large onions, chopped
1 green bell pepper, julienned
1 red bell pepper, julienned
2 medium tomatoes, diced, or ¹/₂ cup Tomato Sauce (page 186)
Salt
Sugar
4 large eggs, lightly beaten (optional)
2 tablespoons chopped flat-leaf parsley

1. In a shallow bowl, cover the fish with cold water. Refrigerate the fish for 24 to 36 hours, changing the water every 8 hours or so. Drain the fish, and pat it dry.

2. Lay the cod pieces in a skillet large enough to hold them in a single layer. Add enough olive oil to cover the fish. Bring the fish to a simmer, and cook it for 5 to 10 minutes, until the cod is tender and flaky (do not let the oil get hot enough to boil). Drain the fish, reserving 10 tablespoons of the oil, and let the cod cool.

3. Return the reserved oil to the skillet, and heat it over medium heat. Add the garlic, and cook it for about 3 minutes, until it is browned. Add the onions and peppers, reduce the heat to low, and sauté for about 15 minutes, until the onions have softened. Add the dried tomatoes or Tomato Sauce, stir well, and season to taste with salt and sugar. Cook, stirring occasionally, for 10 to 15 minutes longer, until the flavors blend.

4. While the sauce cooks, remove the skin from the cod, and then carefully lift out any bones. Shred the cod flesh, and add it to the skillet. Stir well, and cook over medium heat for about 10 minutes longer, stirring, until the contents are well mixed and the cod is heated through. A minute or two before serving, add the eggs. Cook, stirring, until the eggs are scrambled and well mixed with the cod and vegetables. Sprinkle with the chopped parsley, and serve immediately.

NOTE: *If you have Biscayne Sauce (page 187) left over from another dish, add ¹/₂ cup to the skillet when you add the tomatoes (or Tomato Sauce) for an even richer flavor.*

❧ *As you have* no doubt noticed, I use parsley in many first-course and main-course recipes. So do all Basque cooks. Using parsley—mainly the flat-leaf kind—is a deeply rooted tradition in Basque cuisine. It's the parsley that makes *salsa verde verde* (green). When my daughter Maria was a small child, she spent a lot of time with my mother while I attended lectures at the university. A great deal of this time was spent in the kitchen, where the little girl "helped" her grandmother cook. She was quite proud of her kitchen skills, and, given the slightest opportunity, listed the ingredients in any dish they had made—always ending with the phrase, ". . . *y un poquito de perejil*" (". . . and a little parsley"). How well she had learned!

Lightly Fried Kokotxas
❧ KOKOTXAS REBOZADAS ❧

Serves 4

Kokotxas are small, flavorful chunks of fish cut from the tip of the lower jaw of cod or hake. In some American fish markets kokotxas are labeled "cod tongue," but they are actually cut apart from the tongue. They can be hard to find in the United States; you may have to ask a few fishmongers before you have success. If you travel in the Basque Country, though, you can order kokotxas at nearly any bar or restaurant. So desirable are these morsels that they often are removed from the fish while still at sea and sold right from the boat as soon as it docks.

1 pound fresh hake or salt cod kokotxas (see Note)
Salt
3 tablespoons unbleached all-purpose flour
2 large eggs, lightly beaten
½ cup olive oil

1. If the kokotxas are salted, lay them in a shallow bowl, and cover them with cold water. Refrigerate the kokotxas for 24 to 36 hours, changing the water every 8 hours or so. Drain the kokotxas, and pat them dry. (If you are using fresh hake kokotxas, skip this step.)

2. Sprinkle the kokotxas with salt and flour, and shake off the excess flour. Pour the eggs into a shallow bowl.

3. In a large skillet, heat the oil over medium-high heat. Dip a few of the kokotxas into the egg, and then add them to the pan. Reduce the heat to medium, and fry the kokotxas for 2 minutes on each side or until they are lightly browned. Lift them from the pan with a slotted spoon, and drain them on two layers of paper towels. Fry the remaining kokotxas the same way. Serve them hot.

NOTE: *Portuguese markets with good fish departments sell kokotxas, labeled as tongues. If they are from cod, they are nearly always salted; if they are from hake, they are fresh. Most kokotxas available in the United States are salted. You can use salted kokotxas to make salt cod dishes such as Salt Cod Pil Pil (page 151).*

Leek-Shrimp Terrine from the House of Bornechea

❖ PASTEL DE PUERRO BORNECHEA ❖

Serves 6 to 8

first tasted this savory terrine at the home of the Bornecheas, a large family with impeccable culinary traditions whom I have known for years. Since the Bornecheas always serve wonderful food, it is a joy to visit them. Here leeks, a popular vegetable in the Basque Country, are combined with shrimp for a modern and elegant main-course dish. It is perfect for warm-weather entertaining, because it can be made well ahead of time and then served at room temperature. Note that this recipe calls for butter, which is rarely used in traditional Basque cooking.

¼ cup (½ stick) unsalted butter
6 leeks (see page 68), white part only, sliced
1 cup dry white wine
1 cup whole milk
2 tablespoons cornstarch
*7 ounces medium shrimp ("U36" or "36-count"), peeled and cut into
bite-sized pieces*
Salt and fresh-ground black pepper
5 large eggs, lightly beaten
Green- or red-leaf lettuce
Homemade (page 184) or commercial mayonnaise

1. Preheat the oven to 375°F. Lightly butter an 8-by-5-inch loaf mold.
2. In a small pot, melt the butter over medium-high heat. Add the leeks, and cook them for 3 to 4 minutes, until they are golden. Add the wine, and cook over medium-low heat for about 15 minutes, until the leeks are tender and the wine is nearly evaporated.
3. Transfer the leeks to a blender or a food processor fitted with a metal blade, add ½ cup of the milk, and purée the mixture. Return it to the pan.

4. In a small bowl, stir the cornstarch into the remaining ½ cup milk.

5. Add the shrimp and the cornstarch mixture to the pan, and bring the contents to a boil over high heat. Immediately reduce the heat to medium-low, and season to taste with salt and pepper. Cook, stirring, for about 5 minutes, until the mixture is thickened.

6. Put the eggs into a heat-proof bowl, and stir the shrimp-vegetable mixture into them, a little at a time to prevent the eggs from cooking. When it is well combined, scrape the mixture into the mold, and cover the mold with aluminum foil. Set the mold in a larger pan, and add enough hot water to come about a third of the way up the side of the mold. Bake the terrine for about 1 hour, until a toothpick inserted near the center comes out clean. Place the mold on a wire rack. Before the terrine cools completely, loosen it by running a knife around the outside of the mold. Let the terrine finish cooling.

7. When the terrine is completely cool, place a flat plate over the mold, and invert the terrine to unmold it. Slice it, and serve the slices at room temperature on lettuce leaves with mayonnaise on the side.

NOTE: *Once the terrine is unmolded, it can be refrigerated for up to 24 hours, covered with plastic wrap.*

Grilled Prawns

❖ LANGOSTINOS A LA PLANCHA ❖

Serves 4

These prawns are not actually grilled, but are quickly cooked in a very hot pan, which leaves them juicy and delicious. I raise and lower the heat several times during cooking to insure that they cook perfectly, and I do not shell them. Instead, I let my guests shell them at the table. I suggest serving these with noth-

continued

ing more than a green salad and some good bread. Be sure to have plenty of napkins on hand, because the shrimp taste best when eaten with your fingers instead of knives and forks.

³/₄ cup olive oil
Juice of 1 lemon
2 teaspoons coarse salt
2 pounds large shrimp, in the shell (see Notes)

1. In a glass or ceramic bowl, whisk together the oil, the lemon juice, and the salt. Add the shrimp, and marinate them for only 1 to 2 minutes.
2. Heat a large skillet over high heat until it is very hot. Lay a single layer of shrimp in the pan, and cook them for 1 minute. Reduce the heat to medium, and cook them for 1 minute longer. Raise the heat to high again, turn the shrimp, and cook them for 1 minute. Reduce the heat to medium, and cook for another minute, until the shrimp are pink. Lift the shrimp from the pan with a slotted spoon, set them aside, and cover them to keep them warm. Cook the remaining shrimp in the same way.
3. Arrange five shrimp on each plate to form a star, with the head ends meeting in the center of the plates. Serve immediately.

NOTES: *For this dish I buy "U10," or "10-count," shrimp, which means there are 10 shrimp per pound, or unit.*

   In the Basque Country we cook prawns with the heads still attached, but you can also make this dish with headless shrimp.

Pan-Fried Fresh Anchovies

❖ ANCHOAS FRESCAS REBOZADAS ❖

Serves 4

The Basques are fortunate to live by the Bay of Biscay, one of the best places in the world for anchovy fishing. This means we commonly eat fresh anchovies— tender little treats indeed. In the United States, anchovies are most often found canned, packed in salt and oil. Even when you find a fishmonger who advertises fresh anchovies, he may actually be selling fresh sardines (immature pilchards), which closely resemble anchovies. If you find either fresh anchovies or small sardines, try this little meal. It's perfect for a light summer meal, and leftover anchovies are great the next day topping a slice of crusty bread for a *bocadillo*—the Spanish version of a sandwich.

1 pound fresh anchovies, cleaned (see Notes)
Salt
3 tablespoons unbleached all-purpose flour
2 large eggs, lightly beaten
½ cup plus 2 tablespoons olive oil

1. Lightly sprinkle the anchovies with salt and then with flour. Shake off any excess flour.
2. Put the eggs into a shallow bowl. Dip the anchovies in the egg.
3. In a large skillet, heat the oil over high heat. Add a single layer of anchovies, reduce the heat to medium, and cook for 1 minute. Raise the heat to high, turn the anchovies over, and cook them for about 1 minute longer, until they are cooked through. Remove them with a slotted spoon, and drain them on two layers of paper towels. Cook the remaining anchovies in the same way. Serve the anchovies as soon as they are cooked or at room temperature.

continued

NOTES: *If the fishmonger cleans the anchovies for you, ask him not to separate the fillets. To clean the anchovies yourself, rinse them under running water, cut off the heads, split the fish open along the bellies, and remove the innards. Carefully lift the central bone from the fish, but do not separate the fillets. Pat them dry with a paper towel.*

You can substitute small fresh sardines for the anchovies.

BOCADILLOS

❧ *In the Basque Country* we are fond of *bocadillos*, our version of the American sandwich. But Basque bocadillos are never made on pre-sliced supermarket breads; we use baguettes or rolls only. We do not toast the bread, nor do we slather it with mayonnaise or mustard. Bocadillos are made with just about any sort of cold meat or fish, with a preference given to those that have been breaded and pan-fried, because this method of preparation keeps the food moist. Cheese and cold omelets are popular for bocadillos, too—the most common omelets for these sandwiches are French (plain) omelets or potato omelets.

We eat bocadillos for *merienda*, a late-day snack or very light meal usually taken when the children come home from school (about 5:00 P.M. in Spain) or when we come in from the office. This is because dinner is eaten far later than it is in the United States, and the merienda staves off hunger. We also take bocadillos with us when we hike, go on a long car trip, or picnic in the countryside.

Trout Navarra-Style

❧ TRUCHA A LA NAVARRA ❧

Serves 4

avarra, a region neighboring the Basque Country, has no seacoast but is blessed with fantastic rivers—some rushing, some deep and slow-moving, and all fed by streams and brooks filled with fish. It should be no surprise, therefore, that when we cook trout in the Basque Country, we use a method common in Navarra. Brook or rainbow trout are best for this preparation, but lake, brown, or any kind of freshwater trout will taste good, too.

Four ¹/₂ pound trout, cleaned, heads left on
Salt
Juice of ¹/₂ lemon
¹/₄ cup olive oil
5 thin slices serrano ham, prosciutto, or bacon
2 tablespoons unbleached all-purpose flour
2 garlic cloves, chopped
2 tablespoons chopped flat-leaf parsley

1. Preheat the oven to 500°F.
2. Lightly sprinkle the trout inside and out with salt. Sprinkle the lemon juice inside the trout. Set the trout aside for about 10 minutes.
3. In a skillet large enough to hold four trout, heat the oil over medium-high heat. Cook four slices of ham for 1 to 2 minutes, just until they are lightly browned. Drain them briefly on paper towels, and then put a slice inside each trout. Keep the pan warm on the stove.
4. Spread the flour on a plate or in a shallow dish. Coat the fish with flour, and immediately place them in the pan. Raise the heat to high, and cook the trout for about 3 minutes on each side, until they are golden brown but not completely cooked. With a slotted spoon, transfer the fish to a shallow casserole. Keep the pan warm on the stove.

continued

5. Finely chop the remaining slice of ham. Add the ham and garlic to the pan, and cook them over medium-high heat for 3 to 4 minutes, until the ham is lightly browned and the garlic is softened. Spoon the ham, garlic, and oil over the trout.

6. Bake the trout for 5 minutes or until they are cooked through. Sprinkle them with the parsley, and serve immediately.

Red Snapper Guernica-Style

❖ BESUGUITO GUERNICA ❖

Serves 4

A popular fish in the United States, red snapper reminds me very much of our *besugo*, which is actually sea bream. Cooking snapper in a hot oven and then topping it with garlicky oil, as we do besugo in the Basque Country, brings out the mild sweetness of the fish.

Four ³/₄-pound red snapper fillets, skin on (from two 2-pound fish)
Salt
¹/₄ cup plus 2 tablespoons olive oil
2 garlic cloves, sliced thin
1 teaspoon hot red pepper flakes
1 tablespoon sherry vinegar
2 tablespoons chopped flat-leaf parsley

1. Preheat the oven to 500°F.

2. Lay the fillets, skin-side down, on a lightly oiled baking pan. Sprinkle the fillets lightly with salt, and bake them for about 10 minutes, or until the fish is opaque throughout. Transfer the fillets to a hot platter.

3. In a small skillet or saucepan, heat the oil over medium heat. Add the garlic, and cook it for 3 to 4 minutes, until it is golden. Raise the heat to

medium-high, and add the pepper flakes and vinegar. Take care—the vinegar may cause the contents of the pan to flare. Cook, stirring, for about 10 seconds, until the sauce is blended.

4. Spoon the sauce over the fillets, and garnish them with parsley. Serve immediately.

Red Snapper with Piquillo Sauce

◆ BESUGUITO CON SALSA DE PIQUILLO ◆

Serves 4

If you are in the Basque Country, be sure to visit Bermeo, a picturesque fishing village between Bilbao and San Sebastián (or Donostia, in Euskera) where every boat in the small harbor is painted bright red, blue, or green. At the docks you can detect the clean, briny smell of fresh shrimp, tuna, silvery anchovies, and other fish that are unloaded daily in this busy little town. Immediately upon unloading, the seafood and fish are carted to the *cofradía*, the wholesale fish market directly opposite the docks. In every restaurant and bar in Bermeo you can sample different kinds of fish, often grilled over outdoor braziers. A favorite is *besuguito*, for which red snapper is a close and delicious substitute.

3 scallions, minced
1 tomato, diced fine
1 teaspoon drained small capers (optional)
2 tablespoons extra-virgin olive oil
1 tablespoon sherry vinegar
1 cup Piquillo Pepper Sauce (page 190)
Four ¾-pound red snapper fillets, skin on (from two 2-pound fish)
Salt

continued

1. Preheat the oven to 500°F. Lightly oil a baking sheet.

2. In a small bowl, combine the scallions, tomato, capers (if you're using them), olive oil, and vinegar, and stir gently to mix. Set the bowl aside.

3. In a small saucepan, heat the piquillo sauce over medium heat until it is hot but not boiling. Remove the pan from the heat, and cover it to keep the sauce warm.

4. Lightly sprinkle the fillets with salt, and lay them skin-side down on the baking sheet. Bake them for 10 to 12 minutes, until they are opaque and just beginning to flake.

5. Put a fillet on each of four plates. Spoon the warm sauce over each fillet, and garnish with the vinaigrette.

BESUGO

❧ *In the Basque* Country, we often cook a fish called *besugo*, which I have not found in the United States. Besugo is a delicious treat eaten around Christmastime in Spain (not just in the Basque Country), when it is plentiful in the waters.

To me, red snapper most closely approximates the lovely, delicate flavor of besugo, although you could instead substitute porgy, a smaller fish that in Spain is sometimes used instead of besugo.

Pan-Seared Turbot

❖ RODABALLO A LA PLANCHA ❖

Serves 4

To choose my favorite fish would be a very tough decision, but my choice would probably be turbot. Considered "king of the flatfishes," turbot is priced accordingly high (if you see turbot priced lower than sole, avoid it; most likely it isn't really turbot). Turbot are larger and rounder than sole with somewhat rough, brownish-grey skin on the upper part and smooth, nearly white skin on the underside. Although they can grow to 40 pounds, turbot are usually sold at 2 to 8 pounds. I suggest buying 4-pound turbot for the sweetest, whitest, firmest meat.

Because turbot is so delicious, I don't like to mask its flavor with any kind of sauce. Try it cooked in a very hot pan, as I describe here. It's important to raise and lower the heat as instructed to insure properly cooked fish.

¾ cup olive oil, plus a little more
Juice of 1 lemon, plus a little more
2 teaspoons coarse salt
Two 4-pound turbots, filleted, skin on (see Note)

1. In a shallow dish, gently whisk together the ¾ cup olive oil, the juice of one lemon, and the salt.
2. Set one large or two medium skillets over high heat, and heat them until they are very hot.
3. Dip the fillets in the oil mixture, and lay them in the pan, skin side up. Sear them for 1 minute. Reduce the heat to medium-high, and cook the fillets for 2 minutes longer. Raise the heat to high, carefully turn the fillets with a flat spatula, and cook them for 1 minute. Reduce the heat to medium, and cook the fillets for 2 minutes more.
4. Serve the fillets immediately on heated plates, with a little lemon juice and olive oil sprinkled over them.

continued

Fish and Seafood ❖ 167

Baked Salmon with Vinaigrette

◆ SALMON AL HORNO CON VINAGRETA ◆

Serves 4

Wild salmon, hatched in rivers, spend most of their lives in the ocean. When the time to spawn (lay eggs) arrives, they swim back up the rivers. After laying and fertilizing the eggs, the salmon die. During the migration, sport fishermen angle for the fish, which, just caught, are indescribably delicious. Since wild salmon are becoming increasingly rare, however, most salmon sold in markets is farm-raised. Farmed fish, which spend their lives in salt water, are very good, too, particularly when cooked this way. This dish must be prepared at the last minute, but it is very easy.

One 2- to 3-pound salmon fillet
Salt
1 tomato, diced fine
3 scallions, chopped
2 tablespoons extra-virgin olive oil
1 tablespoon sherry vinegar
½ recipe Home-Style Roasted Potatoes (page 197)
Mixed salad greens
House Vinaigrette (page 184)

1. Preheat the oven to 500°F. Lightly rub a baking sheet with olive oil.
2. Cut the fillet into four pieces of equal size, and sprinkle salt on both sides. Lay the pieces on the baking sheet.

3. In a small bowl, combine the tomato, scallions, oil, and vinegar, and mix well. Spoon the mixture evenly over the salmon, and bake it about 10 minutes for medium-rare fish. For rare fish bake it for 5 to 7 minutes, and for better-done fish bake it for 12 minutes.

4. Spoon potatoes into the center of each plate, and top with a piece of salmon. Surround with salad greens, drizzled with a little vinaigrette.

Red Mullet Santurce-Style

❖ SALMONETES AL ESTILO DE SANTURCE ❖

Serves 4

Red mullet, imported from Europe to the United States, are not available at all fish markets. But if you can find them, try them. They are small fish, ranging from 4 to 8 ounces each, and are intensely red or salmon-colored. I call these "Santurce-style" because I always order them cooked this way at a tavern in the port town of Santurce. We usually eat them with no accompaniment, using our fingers or forks to separate the fish from the tiny bones. If you do not want to bother with the bones, ask the fishmonger to fillet the fish, and prepare them as I do the Baked Salmon with Vinaigrette (page 168), reducing the baking time by half.

4 to 8 red mullets (1 to 1½ pounds total), cleaned, heads on
Salt
3 tablespoons unbleached all-purpose flour
½ cup olive oil

1. Lightly sprinkle the mullets inside and out with salt. Spread the flour on a plate, and coat the fish on both sides with flour. Shake off the excess.

2. In a skillet, heat the oil over high heat. Fry the fish for 1 minute. Reduce the heat to medium-high, turn the fish, and fry them for 2 to 3 minutes longer if they're small, or about 5 minutes if they're large. Drain them on two layers of paper towels. Serve the fish hot.

❧ *Anyone who has* fished for albacore tuna, or *bonito*, as we Basques call it, will agree that this is an exhilarating experience—providing the weather is good. During the summer, my friends and I would set off to fish for tuna at four in the morning so that we would be far enough out on the waters by daybreak to find the schools of magnificent leaping fish. Basques call *bonito* "vagabonds of the seas" because each year they travel great distances: In the spring they form schools in the Gulf of Biscay, and in summer they come closer to shore. In fall and winter, they swim in far deeper waters. It's a glorious spectacle when the silver-blue fish leap from the foam they create as they slap the surface of the water, chasing schools of smaller fish and moving like quicksilver through the waves. From above the blue water, sea birds also attack the smaller fish. The entire scene is one of nature's most powerful ballets.

Tuna Steaks with Caramelized Onion
❖ ATÚN O BONITO ENCEBOLLADO ❖

Serves 4

Over the years, the Basques have developed a number of ways of preparing the abundant *bonito*, or albacore tuna, in our waters. This is one of my favorites.

4 tuna steaks, about 8 ounces each (see Note)
Salt
½ cup plus 2 tablespoons olive oil
3 medium onions, sliced thin
1 green bell pepper, cut into thin strips
2 tablespoons brandy

1. Sprinkle both sides of the tuna steaks with salt, and set them aside.
2. In a large skillet, heat ½ cup of the oil over medium-high heat. Add the onions and pepper, and sauté them for about 5 minutes. Reduce the heat, and cook them over medium-low heat for about 20 minutes, until the onions are very soft. Add the brandy, and mix well. Remove the pan from the heat.
3. In another skillet, heat the remaining 2 tablespoons olive oil over high heat. Add the tuna steaks, and sear them for about 1 minute on each side. Transfer the tuna to the skillet with the vegetables, and cook, uncovered, over medium-low heat for 5 minutes (for medium-rare fish) or longer, until the tuna is done to your liking. Spoon the onions and pepper over the steaks, and serve.

NOTE: Bonito, *or albacore tuna, should not be confused with American bonito, a different, darker-fleshed species that cannot be legally labeled as tuna.*

Tuna Breast with Vegetable Stew

❖ VENTRESCA DE ATÚN CON PISTO ❖

Serves 4

If you're visiting the Basque Country during the summer, you most likely will be served albacore tuna, which we call *bonito*. It is far smaller than other tuna, and its breast is especially juicy and tasty. In the United States, this choice part is often called the belly rather than the breast, but regardless of the moniker it is hard to

continued

find (most albacore breast is sold to the Japanese for sashimi and sushi). This dish is very good with other tuna, too, although they are red-fleshed rather than white, as is albacore. I like to serve this with Vegetable Stew (page 51) or other vegetables.

2 tablespoons olive oil
2 pounds tuna breast (belly), preferably, or tuna steak, cut into 4 pieces
Salt
2 garlic cloves, minced

1. Preheat the oven to 500°F. Rub a baking pan with the olive oil.
2. Lightly sprinkle the skinless surfaces of the tuna with salt, and rub them with garlic. Lay the tuna pieces in the baking pan, skin-side down, and bake them for about 15 minutes without turning them. Serve them immediately. (Do not eat the skin; it is tough.)

Baked Striped Bass

◆ LUBINA AL HORNO ◆

Serves 4

Lubina, or sea bass, is difficult to get in the United States, so here I use striped bass. It is a wonderful fish, although it's often hard to find in small sizes. If you cannot locate a 4-pound fish, buy the tail end of a larger bass. Buy it whole, not filleted, with the bone still in the center. Or substitute a whole red snapper for the striped bass in this recipe.

One 4-pound striped bass, cleaned and scaled, head on
¼ cup olive oil
Salt
½ lemon, cut into 4 thin wedges
3 medium potatoes, peeled and sliced thin
1 tablespoon dry bread crumbs
1 tablespoon chopped flat-leaf parsley

1. Preheat the oven to 450°F. Rub the baking pan with 2 tablespoons of the oil.
2. Lightly sprinkle the bass inside and out with salt. Using a sharp knife, make two crosswise slits on each side of the fish, and insert a lemon slice in each.
3. Lay the potatoes in a single layer in the baking pan. Lightly sprinkle them with salt. Lay the striped bass on the potatoes, drizzle the fish with the remaining 2 tablespoons oil, and sprinkle with the bread crumbs and parsley. Bake the fish for about 40 minutes, or 10 minutes per pound. Serve the fish hot with the potatoes, removing the bones carefully.

Grouper Bilbao-Style
❖ MERO A LA BILBAÍNA ❖

Serves 4

In Basque cuisine, the term *bilbaína* refers to a green sauce (*salsa verde*) that contains asparagus, green peas, and hard-cooked eggs. A Basque woman named Placida de Larrea developed this sauce in 1723, so it is as much a classic as well-known French sauces, such as hollandaise and bearnaise. Because of the outstanding reputation of Bilbao's food, however, some cooks and chefs call other sauces *bilbaína* simply for prestige.

I love grouper with this sauce, but you could also use hake, monkfish, or any other white fish. The sauce does not work well with oilier, darker-fleshed fishes such as tuna or salmon.

continued

2 pounds grouper fillets, cut into 16 pieces
Salt
About 1 cup unbleached all-purpose flour
12 Manila, littleneck, or cherrystone clams, well scrubbed (see Note)
2 cups water
½ cup olive oil
2 garlic cloves, minced
½ cup minced flat-leaf parsley
½ cup dry white wine
1 can (8 pieces) white asparagus, preferably from Navarra, drained, or
8 spears cooked fresh white asparagus
½ cup cooked green peas
2 hard-cooked eggs, each cut into 4 wedges

1. Sprinkle the grouper with salt. Spread the flour on a plate, and coat the fish with it on all sides. Shake off the excess flour, and set the fish aside.

2. In a large saucepan, combine the clams and water, and bring the water to a boil over high heat. Reduce the heat to medium-low, and boil for about 5 minutes, until the clams open. Drain them, using a fine-mesh sieve, and reserve ½ cup of the cooking liquid. Discard any clams that have not opened.

3. In a large flame-proof earthenware casserole or skillet, heat the olive oil over medium heat. Add the garlic, and sauté it for about 1 minute, until it is light golden. Arrange the grouper pieces in a single layer in the casserole or skillet, and cook them over medium heat for about 2 minutes on each side. Add the parsley, the wine, and the reserved clam cooking liquid, and cook for 1 to 2 minutes, gently shaking the pan to prevent sticking. Add the clams, asparagus, and peas, and simmer for about 3 minutes longer, until the clams and vegetables are heated through. Remove the casserole or skillet from the heat, add the egg wedges, and serve immediately.

NOTE: *You should be able to get Manila clams from a reputable fishmonger, although you may have to special-order them. If they are not available, use littleneck or slightly larger cherrystone clams. Cockles are a good substitute, too, although they may be hard to find.*

❧ *Getaria is a* well-known fishing town that is almost an obligatory stop when visiting the Basque Country. Close to San Sebastián (Donostia, in Euskera), it is easy to find. Getaria is not only the birthplace of the sixteenth-century global navigator Juan Sebastián Elcano, but also the site of the acclaimed Txomin Etxaniz vineyards. The largest producer of *txakolí*—a mildly effervescent white wine that is a wonderful accompaniment for fish and seafood—the winery is well worth visiting. Getaria's restaurants are first-rate, and its harbor picturesque. Kaia, an excellent harborside restaurant, is a perfect perch from which to watch the fishing boats come and go and unload their daily catch.

Baby Squid in Black Ink Sauce
❧ CHIPIRONES EN SU TINTA ❧

Serves 4

This is among the most typical of Basque dishes. The squid ink turns the dish completely black, which may look a little strange to the uninitiated, but the delicate flavor of the ink makes the dish an immediate winner. When I was a girl, we spent the summers in the fishing village of Mundaka. My father, who loved to fish, often caught so much that even our large family could not eat all his catch. I recall waiting at the port for my father's boat, and then taking buckets of squid and fish to distribute to my father's numerous friends. I was often tipped very generously by these friends, who provided a secret income that I did not declare to the "paternal IRS."

continued

1 cup olive oil

2 medium onions, chopped

1 red onion, chopped

2 leeks (see page 68), white part only, sliced thin crosswise

1 garlic clove, minced

1 tablespoon chopped parsley

1 medium tomato, peeled and chopped

24 small (baby) squid (no more than 2½ inches long, measured without
tentacles), cleaned (see page 177)

Salt

2 tablespoons squid ink (see Note)

3 cups cooked white rice

1. In a large skillet, heat the olive oil over low heat, and cook the onions, leeks, garlic, parsley, and tomato for about 10 minutes, until the onions and leeks soften and turn almost transparent and the tomato releases its liquid.

2. Turn the squid inside out, and insert the winglets, heads, and tentacles of the squid into the body cavities, making small packages.

3. Add a few squid to the pan, and cook them for about 5 minutes on each side, sprinkling them lightly with salt. Using tongs, gently lift the squid from the pan. Drain them in a strainer, pressing gently to remove excess liquid. Transfer them to a flame-proof casserole. Cook the remaining squid in the same way.

4. Add the squid ink to the pan, and boil the mixture over high heat, stirring, for about 10 minutes, until it is blended and black. Transfer the contents of the pan to a blender or food processor fitted with a metal blade, and blend until the sauce is smooth.

5. Pour the sauce over the squid, and bring the squid and its sauce to a simmer over medium heat. Cook for about 5 minutes, until the dish is heated through. Serve it with the rice.

NOTE:

Squid ink is sold frozen in plastic bags in good fish markets and some specialty-foods stores. You can, of course, use the ink from the squid, but you will need more squid—perhaps twice as many. A more practical substitute might be cuttlefish ink, which is very similar to squid ink. For 1 tablespoon ink, you'll need just one or two cuttlefish.

❖ *Squid are plentiful* in ocean waters, Atlantic and Pacific. They are inexpensive, too. As when selecting any seafood, though, be sure the squid you buy smells fresh and slightly briny.

Cleaning squid, though not complicated, is generally the most time-consuming part of preparing any squid dish. If you prefer to avoid the task, buy frozen squid already cut into rings, and use them instead. The dish will not be quite the same, but it will still taste good, since freezing doesn't alter the texture of squid. You will need 2 pounds of squid rings to substitute for 24 baby squid.

To clean squid yourself, hold them over a colander, and rinse them under cold running water. Peel the pale brown skin from the body to expose the white flesh. Carefully tear off the winglets, and drop them into the colander (unless you are making Pan-Seared Baby Squid, page 00, in which case you should leave the winglets intact). Separate the head and tentacles from the body, and peel as much skin from the tentacles and head as possible. Discard the mouth (a tiny round opening) and eyes; use care when removing them (or discard the entire heads, if you prefer). Drop the peeled tentacles and head into the colander. Remove and discard the hard "pen" and all soft parts from inside the body. Turn the body inside out, and rinse the squid well. This step is important because it allows thorough cleaning of the inside and because it causes the cavity opening to shrink during cooking so that the stuffing (tentacles, winglets, and head) is held inside the body. If you're making Pan-Seared Baby Squid, turn each body right side out again.

If you want to use the squid's own ink, locate the gland among the soft parts of the body, and carefully separate it. Otherwise, discard the gland and use store-bought squid ink; it is available frozen at some fish markets and specialty-foods stores.

Insert the winglets, head, and tentacles into the body cavity, making a small package. With practice, cleaning time per squid should be about 3 to 4 minutes.

Squid Pelayo

❖ CHIPIRONES PELAYO ❖

Serves 4

In the port town of Getaria, squid are often cooked the traditional Basque way, in black ink sauce. But nearly as often they are sautéed in olive oil with a good amount of chopped onions, which are served spooned over the squid; this dish is called *Chipirones Pelayo*. Maria Angeles, a waitress who works at Kaia, a harbor-side restaurant, explained the name this way: Years ago a local squid fisherman named Pelayo, tiring of the black ink sauce that is so common in Basque cooking, urged his wife to try another method of preparing his catch. She was so successful that the simple preparation was adopted by Kaia and other restaurants in the Basque Country and christened with the fisherman's name. My mother, too, searched for other ways to cook the pounds of squid my father caught during our summer holidays and, on her own, came up with a similar recipe. Her recipe may not be as famous as Pelayo's, but I like it better. See the variation following this recipe.

½ cup olive oil
4 medium onions, cut into strips
24 small (baby) squid (no more than 2½ inches long, measured without tentacles), cleaned (see Note and page 177)
Salt

1. In a large skillet, heat the oil over medium-high heat. Add the onions, and sauté them for about 10 minutes, until they are softened.
2. Lightly sprinkle the squid with salt, and add the squid to the pan, pushing the onions to the side so that the squid touch the bottom of the pan. Cook them for 2 to 3 minutes on each side, until they are lightly browned. Reduce the heat to medium-low, and cook them for about 15 minutes, stirring from time to time, until they are tender and cooked through.
3. Serve the squid topped with the onions from the pan.

NOTE: *You can substitute 2 pounds squid rings, which are available frozen in many supermarkets. Let them thaw in the refrigerator before proceeding with the recipe. The dish won't taste exactly the same, but it will still be delicious.*

VARIATION:

MARICHU'S SAUTÉED SQUID WITH ONIONS
Chipirones Encebollados Marichu

Sauté 2 tablespoons julienned green bell pepper along with the onions. When the vegetables are softened, stir in 2 tablespoons brandy, and heat gently. Cook the squid as indicated but in a separate pan, in 3 to 4 tablespoons of olive oil. Just before serving, add the cooked squid to the pan with the onions and peppers, and heat all the contents through. Serve the squid with the onion-pepper sauce spooned over them.

Pan-Seared Baby Squid
❖ CHIPIRONES A LA PLANCHA ❖

Serves 4

In the Basque Country we eat squid quite often, as do people in most of Spain and the other countries bordering the Mediterranean Sea. In the United States, though, most people rarely think of eating squid, unless it is deep-fried calamari. I hope this will change, because squid really are delicious. For the most tender texture, select the smallest squid possible.

continued

6 tablespoons olive oil

Juice of ½ lemon

1½ teaspoons coarse salt

*24 small (baby) squid (no more than 2½ inches long,
measured without tentacles), cleaned, with winglets left intact and
tentacles separated from the bodies (see page 177)*

FOR THE VINAIGRETTE:

1 medium tomato, diced

3 scallions, diced

3 tablespoons extra-virgin olive oil

1 teaspoon sherry vinegar

Salt

. . .

1 tablespoon chopped flat-leaf parsley

1. To prepare the squid, whisk together the olive oil, lemon juice, and salt in a small, shallow bowl.

2. Heat a large nonstick skillet over high heat. Dip three or four squid bodies or tentacles in the marinade only long enough to coat them. Sear the bodies and tentacles for 1 to 2 minutes on each side, until they are lightly browned. Remove them with tongs, and drain them on two layers of paper towels while searing the remaining squid.

3. Arrange six squid bodies on each plate, and place a set of tentacles at each body opening, so that the squid form a star pattern with the tentacles stretching outward.

4. To prepare the vinaigrette, combine the tomato, scallions, olive oil, and vinegar in a small bowl, and stir gently to mix. Season to taste with salt.

5. Spoon the vinaigrette between the squid on each plate, and garnish with parsley.

Basque Basics

This may seem like an unlikely jumble of recipes—one for mayonnaise, another for vinaigrette, and then more for sauce after sauce—all followed by a few standard broths, a bread, a breakfast cake, two potato side dishes, and the Basque version of applesauce. But these are the basic recipes that every good Basque cook relies on to turn a good meal into a spectacular one, a simple dish into a memorable one.

Here is the vinaigrette that I sprinkle over salads and cold vegetables day in and day out. Here, too, are the chicken, beef, and fish broths I use as the bases for soups, stews, and sauces. And here is a recipe for an odd and old-fashioned Basque hearth bread called talo that belongs in no other chapter but without question belongs in this book.

Much of this chapter is dedicated to sauces. We Basques are justly proud of our sauces, a small but powerful repertoire that gives our cooking the distinction it has earned over the centuries. Our most admired sauce is salsa vizcaína, which I discuss at some length later in this chapter. But we also are acclaimed for our salsa pimientos del piquillo and salsa española, among others. Some of the best-known Basque sauces, those that are intrinsic to certain dishes, must be made at the time of serving, and so are not included here but can be found elsewhere in the book within main-dish recipes. For instance, the black ink sauce that accompanies our prized squid is part of the squid recipe on page 175.

The sauces described in this chapter, however, can be prepared in advance and matched with many foods—fish, meat, and poultry. Every Basque cook has at least one of these sauces on hand in the refrigerator at all times to facilitate family meals and just make life easier. In my case, this sensible habit has enabled me to make last-minute meals that everyone in my family enjoys.

House Vinaigrette

Makes about ¹/₂ cup

I call this classic dressing "house" vinaigrette because I use it over and over at the restaurant and at home. It's made in the classic ratio of three parts oil to one part vinegar—but when we Basques make vinaigrette, we use sherry vinegar rather than red wine vinegar, as do the French. I use this dressing on salad greens and many cold cooked vegetables, such as leeks (see page 68), asparagus, green beans, and artichokes.

2 tablespoons sherry vinegar
¹/₄ cup plus 2 tablespoons extra-virgin olive oil
Salt

Pour the vinegar into a small bowl. Slowly add the oil, whisking constantly until the oil and vinegar are emulsified. Season to taste with salt. Whisk well again just before serving.

Mayonnaise

❖ MAYONESA ❖

Makes about 1¹/₂ cups

As in so many European cuisines, classic mayonnaise is the base for numerous sauces and dressings in the Basque country. Add garlic, herbs, parsley, anchovies, or other seasonings, depending on how the mayonnaise will be served. Note that it is made with raw egg; if this worries you (because of the small risk of salmonella poisoning), use commercial mayonnaise when a recipe calls for *mayonesa*. I include this recipe because I grew up using it—and to leave it out would seem unnatural to me. For success, be sure the egg is at room temperature.

1 large egg, at room temperature
1½ cups extra-virgin olive oil (see Notes)
1 teaspoon salt
1 tablespoon sherry vinegar (see Notes)

1. In a blender, combine the egg with about 1 teaspoon of oil and the salt. Blend at the lowest speed.
2. With the blender still running, add the remaining olive oil in a slow, steady stream until the oil is incorporated. If you prefer a thicker mayonnaise, blend for an additional 10 seconds at a higher speed.
3. Transfer the mayonnaise to a bowl, and stir in the vinegar well. Serve immediately, or refrigerate the mayonnaise, covered, for up to 2 days.

NOTES: *It is easiest to make mayonnaise in a small blender jar or with a hand-held blender in a large cup. You can also do it the old-fashioned way, of course, by using a whisk. Add the oil drop by drop at first, then in a very thin stream, as you whisk constantly.*

For milder tasting, whiter mayonnaise, use corn oil in place of olive oil. You can also substitute lemon juice or another type of vinegar for sherry vinegar.

Spanish Sauce

❖ SALSA ESPAÑOLA ❖

Makes about 2 cups

This very popular brown sauce usually accompanies meat dishes, but it is also delicious with tuna steaks, stuffed peppers, and other dishes. It's easy to make, partially because the ingredients are readily available.

continued

¼ cup olive oil
2 medium onions, chopped
1 medium carrot, sliced
1 garlic clove, sliced
2 tablespoons chopped flat-leaf parsley
2 tablespoons unbleached all-purpose flour
2 cups homemade (page 195) or canned beef broth or water
½ cup dry sherry
Salt

1. In a skillet, heat the olive oil over medium heat. Add the onions, carrot, garlic, and parsley, and sauté for about 10 minutes, until the onions are golden brown.

2. Add the flour, stir well to blend, and cook for about 5 minutes longer, stirring constantly. Add the broth or water a little at a time, stirring constantly. Reduce the heat, and cook for about 20 minutes, until the sauce is well blended and slightly thickened.

3. Add the sherry, and season the sauce to taste with salt. Cook for about 10 minutes longer, until the flavors blend.

4. Pass the sauce through a food mill, or purée it in a blender or food processor. Serve it immediately, or store it in a covered container in the refrigerator for up to 3 days.

Tomato Sauce

❖ SALSA DE TOMATE ❖

Makes about 3 cups

I nearly always have this easy sauce on hand in the refrigerator at home as well as at the restaurant. Because it is a basic ingredient in so many recipes, it has saved me a number of times when I had to cook something without much warning.

I highly recommend using a food mill (see page 87) for this recipe. It produces a sauce with a more authentic, robust consistency and a redder color than does a blender or food processor.

If the fresh tomatoes at the market are not fully ripe, substitute canned tomatoes.

¼ cup olive oil
1 medium onion, chopped
3 pounds (8 to 9) tomatoes, cut into small pieces (see Note)
Salt
Sugar

1. In a skillet, heat the olive oil over low heat. Add the onion, and cook it, stirring occasionally with a wooden spoon, for about 10 minutes, or until the onion is softened.
2. Add the tomatoes, and season to taste with salt and sugar. Stir well, and cook for about 30 minutes, stirring occasionally with the wooden spoon.
3. Pass the sauce through a food mill, or purée it in a blender or food processor. Serve the sauce immediately, or store it in a covered container in the refrigerator for up to 6 days.

NOTE: *If you can't find good ripe tomatoes, substitute about 3¾ cups of drained, peeled (not crushed) canned tomatoes. Canned tomatoes are not as good as seasonal ripe ones, but they are far better than dry, mealy, out-of-season tomatoes.*

Biscayne Sauce

✦ SALSA VIZCAÍNA ✦

Makes 3 cups

Anyone who has traveled in the Basque country has sampled this lovely sauce, since it is probably the most famous of all our sauces. But when I sat down to write the book, I debated including this recipe, despite its importance to Basque cuisine, because *choricero*, the sweet, dried red peppers necessary for it,

continued

are not imported to the United States. I tried making the sauce with other mild, sweet dried red peppers, which are easily available all over the United States, but although flavorful, these do not produce a sauce that tastes authentic to me. Still, I finally decided that it is better to tell you how to make a good approximation of the sauce than to deprive you of the recipe altogether.

8 dried red choricero peppers, or 6 dried red California (Anaheim)
or ancho peppers (see Note)
½ cup olive oil
2 medium yellow onions, chopped
1 medium red onion, chopped
1 garlic clove, sliced
2 tablespoons serrano ham or prosciutto, chopped (optional)
Salt
About ½ cup Tomato Sauce (page 186)

1. Put the peppers into a bowl, and soak them in cold water for at least 8 hours. Transfer the peppers and soaking liquid to a saucepan, and heat them over medium heat until they are simmering, but not boiling. Drain the peppers, reserving 1 cup of the liquid. Slit the peppers open, and scrape out the seeds. Discard the seeds.

2. In a skillet, heat the olive oil over medium heat. Add the onions and garlic, and sauté them for about 5 minutes, until they are softened. Add the peppers and ham, if you're using it, and cook for about 5 minutes, until the peppers begin to soften. Reduce the heat to low, add the reserved cooking liquid, and season to taste with salt. Cook, stirring, for 20 to 30 minutes, until the peppers are very soft and the sauce is slightly reduced.

3. Add the tomato sauce (you may want to add a little more or a little less than ½ cup, according to your taste), and cook for about 5 minutes, until the sauce is hot. Pass it through a food mill, and serve it immediately, or store it in a covered container in the refrigerator for up to 3 days.

NOTE: *Because California and ancho peppers tend to be a little larger than choriceros, I use fewer of them.*

❧ *Salsa Vizcaína is* without doubt the most celebrated Basque sauce. In his book *Bocuse: Cuisine des Regions de France*, Paul Bocuse includes a recipe for *salsa vizcaína* in his chapter on the Bordelaise region; although the sauce originated in the Spanish province of Vizcaya, he explains, it is also appreciated in France.

When a dish is prepared with this full-flavored pepper sauce, it is invariably called "Biscayne-style" (*vizcaína*)—and there are a number of such dishes in this book. Unhappily, the sweet, dried red peppers necessary for an authentic sauce are not imported to the United States, so you may have to substitute others, which will not produce an absolutely authentic-tasting sauce. (Throughout the Caribbean, you will find sauces called Biscayne, but these are all quite different from the traditional Basque version.)

These all-important peppers, called *choriceros*, grow only in the Basque region of Spain. When dried, they are not only used for *salsa vizcaína*, but they are also crushed and mixed with pork to make chorizo sausages, to which they give a characteristic ruddy color. Not only do I rely on choricero peppers for a taste of Spain, but the farm where I buy them, owned by my friend Felisa Madariaga, is absolutely beautiful, and so I always enjoy this particular shopping trip.

Piquillo Pepper Sauce

Serves 4

Basques have only quite recently added cream to sauces, and so this is an example of a modern Basque recipe that has roots in our culinary history. When I was asked to be the guest chef for a gala dinner at New York City's Pierre Hotel honoring Severiano Ballesteros, the acclaimed Spanish golfer, I served this sauce with red snapper. At the restaurant, I serve it often with striped bass, scallops, and other mild-flavored fish.

1¾ cups olive oil
1 medium onion, chopped
1 garlic clove, chopped
8 piquillo peppers; 4 roasted, peeled, and seeded red bell peppers (see page 70);
or 4 canned pimientos, coarsely chopped
3 tablespoons unbleached all-purpose flour
2½ cups Fish Broth (page 196), the saffron omitted
1 cup dry white wine
Salt
1½ cups heavy cream

1. In a saucepan, heat the olive oil over medium heat. Add the onion and garlic, and cook for about 10 minutes, stirring to prevent burning, until the onion softens.

2. Add the peppers, and cook for 5 minutes longer, until they begin to soften.

3. Raise the heat to medium-high, and stir in the flour. Stir until all the ingredients are well mixed. Add the broth and wine, and cook for about 10 minutes, stirring occasionally, until the mixture is heated through. Season to taste with salt, and stir in the cream. Bring the mixture to a simmer, and cook it for about 5 minutes without letting it boil. Transfer it to a blender, and blend the mixture to a purée. Strain the sauce through a fine-mesh sieve, and serve.

❧ *Piquillo is the diminutive* of *pico*, Spanish for "peak." The name is apt, since these triangular peppers end in a very acute point. About 3 inches long, they grow exclusively in Navarra; the best ones come from the subregion of Lodosa. Because piquillos are intensely red when ripe, they are often called Navarra's "red gold."

After the harvest, these peppers are roasted over wood and peeled by hand. For the optimal preservation of their taste and aroma, they are never rinsed in water. At the end of this laborious process, they are sealed in cans or jars with nothing but their own juices.

Because of their high levels of fiber, vitamin C, and carotene, and their low caloric content, piquillos are very healthful. They can be eaten straight from the can with a little vinaigrette, blended in Piquillo Pepper Sauce (page 190), or used in any number of different dishes, such as the ones suggested in this book.

Large specialty-foods stores carry canned piquillo peppers. If you don't have a local source, you can order them from Northern Boulevard, in Queens, New York. The store's telephone number is 718-779-4971.

Cornmeal Skillet Cakes

❖ TALO ❖

Makes about 12 skillet cakes

This is a Basque *caserío*, or "farmhouse," recipe. Whenever I return to the Basque Country, I buy dried red choricero peppers from Felisa Madariaga, who lives on a beautiful farm near Bilbao. She is so generous (and proud that my New York

continued

customers enjoy her peppers) that she always treats me to special dishes, often chorizo sausages and freshly cooked *talo*. *Talo* are similar to Mexican tortillas, but they are a little thicker and more forgiving to make. In the old days, shepherds often carried talo, wrapped around cold meat or some leftover vegetables, into the pastures. Today talo are more often wrapped around sausages. When they are accompanied by a glass of red wine on a cold winter's night, you cannot hope for more!

1 pound yellow or white stone-ground (whole, coarse) cornmeal
Pinch of salt
2 cups very hot water
Olive oil

1. In a large bowl, whisk together the cornmeal and salt. Mound the mixture in the bowl, then make a well in the center of the mound. Pour the hot water into the well. Using your fingers and working outward from the well, mix to make a soft dough that does not stick to your fingers.
2. On a work surface lightly dusted with cornmeal or flour, roll the dough to a thickness of ¼ inch. Using a large biscuit cutter or a small sharp knife, cut out 4-inch rounds.
3. Pour into a skillet just enough oil to coat the bottom. Heat the skillet over high heat, then reduce the heat to medium. Cook the cornmeal rounds for 2 to 3 minutes on each side, until they are golden brown. Drain them on paper towels, and serve them hot or warm.

Breakfast Sponge Cake
❖ BIZCOCHO DE DESAYUNO ❖

Serves 6

When I cook at home, my youngest son, Lucas, loves to be involved, and he often insists on preparing this easy cake. Except for putting it in and taking it from the oven, he can make the entire cake by himself. I have to clean up after him, but his feeling of accomplishment is well worth the extra dusting of flour in the kitchen.

2 large eggs
1 teaspoon finely minced lemon zest
1 cup sugar
1 cup heavy cream
1½ cups unbleached all-purpose flour
1 teaspoon baking powder

1. Preheat the oven to 300°F. Generously butter a large loaf pan (approximately 10 by 6 by 2½ inches) or an 8-inch-square baking pan, and dust it with flour. Tap out the excess flour.

2. In a large mixing bowl, beat the eggs with the zest. Add the cup of sugar, the cream, 1 cup of the flour, and the baking powder. Using a wire whisk, blend the contents. Still whisking, add the remaining ½ cup flour. Whisk until the flour is well incorporated. Scrape the batter into the pan.

3. Bake the cake on the center rack of the oven for 45 minutes. Raise the oven temperature to 350°F, and bake the cake for about 30 minutes longer, until the edges pull away from the sides of the pan and the top is golden. (Check the cake often during the last 15 minutes of baking, in case your oven is hotter than average.)

4. Let the cake cool in its pan on a wire rack. When the cake is cool, turn it out, and serve it at room temperature.

BASQUE BREAKFAST

❖ *Breakfast in the* Basque country is not the full meal it is in northern Europe. We rarely eat more than a slice of toasted bread accompanied by a cup of strong coffee or tea. On occasion we might indulge in a cake, such as the Breakfast Sponge Cake.

My father still drinks a small glass of olive oil mixed with a little lemon juice for breakfast. We were never obliged to follow suit, but he encouraged us by saying, "*Si quieres llegar a viejo, guarda aceite en el pellejo.*" Translation: "If you want to get old, store some olive oil in your skin."

Chicken Broth

Makes about 1 gallon

To make chicken broth in the restaurant, we roast the bones, strain the broth several times, and clarify it—but all of these steps are unnecessary for home cooks. Homemade broth is really quite easy to make, and it tastes so good. When you do not have time to make broth, however, you can use a high-quality canned broth, or even bouillon cubes.

¼ cup olive oil
Bones from 2 uncooked chickens, coarsely chopped
2 whole chicken breasts
2 medium carrots, coarsely chopped
2 leeks, green parts only, coarsely chopped
1 bunch flat-leaf parsley
About ½ cup dried chickpeas
Salt

1. In a stockpot, heat the olive oil over high heat. Add the chopped chickens and cook them, stirring, for about 10 minutes, until they are lightly browned on all sides.

2. Add the chicken breasts, carrots, leeks, parsley, chickpeas, and about 2 gallons (8 quarts) of water. Bring the contents to a boil over high heat. Skim any foam that rises to the surface, reduce the heat to medium, and simmer for about 3 hours, uncovered, until the liquid is reduced by about half. During the simmering, occasionally skim any surface foam.

3. Strain the broth into another pot, discarding the bones and the vegetables. (You may want to use the breast meat to prepare Croquettes; see page 12). Season the broth to taste with salt. Immediately plunge the pot containing the broth into a bowl or sink filled with ice cubes and cold water, and let

the broth cool. Refrigerate or freeze the broth in covered containers until you are ready to use it. The broth will keep in the refrigerator for up to 3 days or in the freezer for up to 1 month.

NOTE: *Chicken broth can be made in a pressure cooker in half the time. Follow the recipe here, but reduce the amount of water to 1 gallon.*

Beef Broth

✦ CALDO DE CARNE ✦

Makes about 1 gallon

When time is short, canned beef broth or even bouillon cubes are usually adequate, but make your own beef broth when you can. Doing so is inexpensive and easy—all you need is time. This broth recipe may be a little different from others you have seen, since it calls for chickpeas and marrow bones. These ingredients, common in the Basque Country, add robust flavor to the broth.

1 beef shank
4 marrow bones (see Notes)
2 knucklebones (see Notes)
1 onion, peeled and halved
2 carrots, coarsely chopped
2 leeks, green parts only, coarsely chopped
1 bunch flat-leaf parsley
About ½ cup dried chickpeas
Salt

1. Rinse the beef shank and bones under running hot water, and put them into a deep stockpot. Add the onion, carrots, leeks, parsley, chickpeas, and

continued

about 2 gallons (8 quarts) of water. Bring the contents to a boil over high heat. Skim any foam that rises to the surface, reduce the heat to medium, and simmer for about 3 hours, uncovered, until the liquid is reduced by about half. During the simmering, occasionally skim any surface foam.

2. Strain the broth into another pot, discarding the bones and the vegetables. (You may want to use the meat from the beef shank to prepare Croquettes; see page 12). Season the broth to taste with salt. Immediately plunge the pot containing the broth into a bowl or sink filled with ice cubes and cold water, and let the broth cool. Refrigerate or freeze the broth in covered containers until you are ready to use it. The broth will keep for up to 3 days in the refrigerator or for up to 1 month in the freezer.

NOTES: *Knucklebones, or knee bones, have a great deal of flavor; although you can use other bones in their place, these sturdy ones are worth hunting for. Marrow bones are usually leg bones. Both knucklebones and marrow bones are often available at supermarkets as well as butcher shops.*

After straining the broth, you can discard the bone marrow along with the bones, but I like it spread on bread or toast with a sprinkling of salt.

Fish Broth

❖ CALDO DE PESCADO ❖

Makes about 7 cups

Provided they are quite fresh, you can use whatever fish bones and shellfish you can easily acquire, or happen to have on hand, for fish broth (also called *fumet*). The only exception is what we call *pescado azul*, blue or oily fishes such as tuna, salmon, sardines, or anchovies. The addition of mollusks, such as clams and mussels, makes this broth especially rich in flavor.

About 1 pound bones of white fish, such as monkfish, cod, or snapper
About 1 cup shrimp shells
1 hake head
10 mussels
10 littleneck or cherrystone clams
1 onion, peeled and halved
1 medium carrot, coarsely chopped
1 bunch flat-leaf parsley
2 quarts water
Salt

1. In a stockpot, combine all of the ingredients. Bring the contents to a boil over high heat. Reduce the heat to low, and simmer gently, uncovered, for about 1 hour.

2. Strain the broth into another pot, and discard the bones, shells, and vegetables. Immediately plunge the pot containing the broth into a bowl or sink filled with ice cubes and cold water, and let the broth cool. Strain it through a fine-mesh sieve, and store it, covered, in the refrigerator or freezer until you are ready to use it. The broth will keep in the refrigerator for up to 3 days or in the freezer for up to 1 month.

Home-Style Roasted Potatoes

❖ PATATAS PANADERAS ❖

Serves 8 to 10

I serve this classic potato dish with any number of main courses—chicken, fish, or beef. Although it is a universal favorite with customers at Marichu, occasionally one asks me if I have a similar dish, perhaps a slight variation on the same theme. I am sure there are many other good potato side dishes, I tell the customer, but why tamper with success? Surely none is as delicious as this one!

continued

4 large potatoes, peeled and cut crosswise ⅛-inch thick
2 red onions, cut into thin strips or rings
¼ cup olive oil
Salt
Ground white pepper (optional)

1. Preheat the oven to 500°F.
2. In a 9-by-13-inch baking dish, combine the potatoes, onions, olive oil, and salt and white pepper (if you're using it) to taste, and toss well. Cover the pan with foil, and bake for about 30 minutes, or until the potatoes are fork-tender and slightly crisp around the edges. Serve immediately.

Basque Fries
❖ PATATAS FRITAS ❖

Serves 4

I invented the term *Basque fries* to contrast these potatoes with French fries. Basque fries are already cooked when submerged in hot oil. After only the briefest time in the oil, they are ready to eat—soft on the inside and crispy and crunchy on the outside. This method uses less oil and avoids any fuss about its temperature.

I serve Basque Fries with meat and fish.

4 small potatoes (about ¾ pound)
½ cup olive oil
Salt

1. Put the potatoes into a saucepan, and add enough water to cover them by several inches. Bring the water to a boil over medium-high heat, reduce the heat to low, and cook the potatoes for about 20 minutes, until they are fork-tender. Drain the potatoes, and set them aside to cool.
2. Peel the potatoes, and cut them into strips or crosswise slices.

3. In a deep skillet, heat the oil over high heat until it is very hot. Add the potatoes, and cook them for about 1 minute, or just until they are golden. Drain them on two layers of paper towels, salt them to taste, and serve them hot.

SPANISH OLIVE OIL

❧ *Since Spain is* the world's largest producer and exporter of olive oil, we Basques have easy access to the golden oil. We use it almost to the exclusion of any other cooking fat (we use lard only occasionally, to rub birds or pork before roasting, and butter only in a very few recipes for baked goods). The flavor of olive oil, which can range from mild to bold and fruity, enhances most of our food; without it, our dishes would not be as good.

The best-tasting olive oil is extra-virgin. The highest quality cold-pressed olive oil, extra-virgin olive oil can appear lusciously green in color. We use it for its delicious flavor in raw preparations and vinaigrettes.

When it is not possible to get extra-virgin oil, virgin olive oil makes a good substitute. For oil to be labeled "virgin," the olives cannot have been stored for longer than two days between harvest and pressing, and no heat can be applied during the pressing process.

For most day-to-day cooking tasks, Basque home cooks use ordinary olive oil. This oil can be made from olives that are not quite as fine as those reserved for extra-virgin and virgin oils, and that may have been stored for a little longer than three days. We rarely use "light" or "extra-light" oil; in fact, these appellations seem to be an American invention. Light olive oils contain just as many calories (nine per gram) as any other vegetable oil, but they are made from oils that have been processed to the point where they are odorless and very pale. These refined oils are then blended with very small amounts of virgin olive oil.

Olive oil is such a common ingredient in Basque kitchens that we rarely worry about how to store it. We pour it into frying pans and over raw foods with judicious audacity, usually keeping a tall bottle fitted with a pouring spout near the work area. I feel olive oil is best if kept in glass bottles, so even when I buy it in large metal cans I transfer it to glass bottles. If you must store olive oil for more than a few months, keep it in a dark, cool place.

Good olive oil is not only delicious; it is also one of the most healthful fats you can use in your daily diet. The International Olive Oil Council is spreading the word about the health benefits of consuming the golden liquid. For nutritional information about olive oil, you can call the council at 800-232-6548 Monday through Friday, 9:00 A.M. to 5:00 P.M. EST.

Potato Purée

❖ PURÉ DE PATATA ❖

Serves 8 to 10

My mother made this potato dish whenever we had an excess of the cream that accumulated at the top of the milk jugs. Today there is no cream at the top of the milk, since milk is homogenized, but I buy heavy cream and make this side dish often. It is similar to American-style mashed potatoes, but it's made with olive oil rather than butter, and it's seasoned with paprika, which colors the potatoes a little. You could halve this recipe, but why bother? Leftovers are great, too.

5 large potatoes, peeled and cut into chunks
Salt
$\frac{1}{2}$ cup olive oil
$\frac{1}{2}$ cup heavy cream
2 teaspoons paprika

1. Put the potatoes into a large saucepan, add enough water to cover them by several inches, and lightly salt it. Bring the water to a boil, reduce the heat to low, and cook the potatoes for about 20 minutes, until they are fork-tender. Drain the potatoes, and pass them through a food mill or mash them with a fork or potato masher. Transfer them to a saucepan.
2. Add the oil in a slow, steady stream, while stirring the potatoes with a spatula or spoon, until all the oil is incorporated. Add the cream in a slow, steady stream, stirring, until it is incorporated too. Season with the paprika and salt. Heat the potatoes gently, and serve immediately.

Apple Purée

◆ PURÉ DE MANZANAS ◆

Serves 4

During the last years of his long life, my grandfather Claudio lived alone in Markina, where he owned several country houses and orchards. He often asked my brother, Manu, to pick the ripe Reineta apples—which are firm, tart, and incredibly delicious—and store them in the attic of one of the houses. When Claudio saw a new crop ripen, he instructed my brother to give away the stored apples to make room for the fresh. This made little sense to my brother, and, since Claudio's mind was not as sharp as it had been, my brother instead gave most of the fresh harvest to my aunts, who lived nearby, without telling my grandfather. My aunts gave many of the apples away, but, even so, they had more than their families could eat raw, and so very often made this apple purée. You

continued

can multiply the ingredients depending on the quantity of apples you have. Serve the purée with pork or game.

3 pounds firm apples, such as Reineta or Fuji, peeled and diced
½ cup water
2 tablespoons sweet Spanish sherry
1 teaspoon sugar
Pinch of salt

1. In a stockpot or large saucepan, combine the apples, water, sherry, sugar, and salt, and bring them to a boil over medium-high heat. Reduce the heat, and simmer for 20 to 30 minutes, until the apples are soft.
2. Pass the mixture through a food mill, or purée it in a blender or food processor until it is smooth and thick. Serve it warm.

Desserts

We Basques eat two three-course meals every day, with the third course being dessert. Although many meals conclude with only a piece of ripe fruit, when a meal ends with a sweet, luscious dessert we are very happy.

Our desserts are simple, homey fare. Most are made with ingredients commonly found in every kitchen—eggs, milk, and sugar—and consequently tend to be smooth, rich, and custardy. Modern desserts

prepared by adventuresome chefs in today's expensive restaurants are perhaps more elegant than these, but I want to share traditional Basque recipes, immediately recognizable by Basques of all generations. So on page 207 you will find a simple custard tart—a recipe my youngest children mastered before I did! Here also are old-fashioned recipes for a creamy rice pudding and a sweet walnut purée, which are nothing if not sinfully good. My favorite dessert, tostadas de crema *(or* leche frita, *"fried milk") is here, too, in all its silken loveliness. This is a treat I rarely had as a child because it is such a bore to prepare, so my otherwise industrious mother usually refused to make it. Still, I ate it whenever possible—it is traditionally served at carnival time in Bilbao—and now I make sure it is always on the restaurant's menu so that I can indulge at whim. And, finally, here is one of our most beloved custard creations, which is also one of the best known. Called* natillas, *it is a thick, ivory-colored sweet cream sauce very similar to what across the border in France is called* crème anglaise.

We like fruit desserts and nut desserts in the Basque Country, too, and so I have included several recipes that illustrate our special ways with apples, figs, pears, quince, almonds, and chestnuts. The quince dessert on page 224 is very interesting because the fruit is cooked until extremely thick and sticky, something not done in very many recipes. And the fig dessert on page 223 is more a celebration of delectable fresh figs than an instruction in cooking, but who cares? Served with natillas, the figs are heavenly.

You will notice that there are no desserts here that could be called cakes, in the American sense, and no chocolate desserts. Although cakes and chocolate desserts are available in the Basque Country, they are not classic Basque preparations. I also left out a typical Basque treat called gatzatu, a farmhouse dessert made from sheep's milk, that resembles sweetened yogurt. Gatzatu is delicious, but because sheep's milk is not easy to get in the United States, I omitted the recipe. If you travel to the Basque Country, I hope you will sample gatzatu, as well as many other desserts, the most traditional of which are included here to provide a sweet overview of how we indulge ourselves in the Basque Country.

Custard Tart Bilbao-Style

✦ TARTA DE ARRESE ✦

Serves 8

This crustless tart is typical of my hometown of Bilbao. Its traditional name, *tarta de arroz*, is misleading, since the tart doesn't contain rice. So I have renamed it in honor of a bakery in Bilbao, Pastelería Arrese, a favorite haunt of mine that makes a delectable version. When I make this tart at the restaurant, I serve it with fresh fruit, a berry coulis, or ice cream.

2 cups whole milk
1 cup unbleached all-purpose flour
3 large eggs, separated
1 cup sugar
½ cup (1 stick) unsalted butter, melted and slightly cooled
1 to 2 cups Sweet Basque Cream (page 208; see Note)

1. Preheat the oven to 350°F. Lightly butter a 9-inch pie plate.

2. In a blender or in a food processor fitted with a metal blade, combine the milk, flour, egg yolks, and sugar. Blend just until the contents are mixed. Transfer them to a bowl.

3. In a separate bowl, whisk the egg whites with a wire whisk to the "snow point"—just until they start to thicken to soft peaks.

4. Gently fold the egg whites and the melted butter into the milk mixture until the whites are almost completely incorporated. Scrape the mixture into the prepared pie plate, and bake it for 45 minutes to 1 hour, until the custard is golden brown and a toothpick inserted near the center comes out clean. Cool the custard on a wire rack until it is just lukewarm. Cut the custard into wedges, and serve them warm or cool. Spoon the Sweet Basque Cream onto the dessert plates, spreading it to cover the plate. Set a wedge of custard on top of the sauce.

NOTE: *The amount of sauce you'll need depends on the size of the dessert plates.*

Sweet Basque Cream

Makes 5 to 6 cups; serves 6

At the restaurant, we offer this sweet, liquid custard as a dessert in itself, served in small custard cups. But *natillas* is also used in countless Basque recipes as a sauce. Although we in the Basque Country claim this sauce as our own, the French make a similar sauce and call it *crème anglaise*—thereby crediting the English as its inventors.

1 quart heavy cream
2 cinnamon sticks
6 large eggs
³/₄ cup sugar
1 tablespoon vanilla extract
Ground cinnamon

1. In a saucepan, combine the cream and cinnamon sticks, and bring them to a boil over medium-high heat. Reduce the heat to low, and cook gently for about 10 minutes, until the cream is well infused with the cinnamon. Set the pan aside so the cream can cool.

2. In a bowl, whisk together the eggs, sugar, and vanilla until they are well mixed. Add the cream and cinnamon sticks, and whisk well.

3. Heat 1 to 2 inches of water in the bottom pan of a double boiler, and transfer the custard mixture to the top pan, or set the bowl over a saucepan containing 1 to 2 inches of hot water. Bring the water to a boil, and cook the sauce, stirring constantly, for about 30 minutes or until it thickens, adding more hot water to the bottom pan if necessary. Remove the top pan or the bowl from over the hot water, and let the custard cool.

4. Strain the cooled custard through a fine-mesh sieve into a glass or ceramic container, and refrigerate the natillas for at least 4 hours, until it is cool. Stir before serving, adding a little more heavy cream if necessary to smooth the natillas. Divide it among six custard cups or transfer it to a pitcher to use as a sauce. Serve the natillas sprinkled with cinnamon.

Basque Tart

Serves 8

Rarely have I come across this dessert in Spain, and I don't recall my mother ever baking it. But it is commonplace in the French Basque country. My cousin Mary, a fine cook in the French tradition who lives in the pretty village of Anglet on the outskirts of Biarritz, gave me the recipe. American readers will consider this more of a tart than a cake, or gateau, despite its traditional name.

FOR THE DOUGH:

1¾ cups unbleached all-purpose flour
¾ cup plus 2 tablespoons sugar
Pinch of salt
1 cup (2 sticks) minus 2 tablespoons unsalted butter, softened
1 large egg
2 large egg yolks
1 teaspoon grated lemon zest
1 teaspoon rum

FOR THE CREAM:

1 cup whole milk
¼ cup sugar
2 tablespoons unbleached all-purpose flour
2 large egg yolks, lightly beaten with a fork
1 teaspoon rum
2 tablespoons raisins (optional)

. . .

1 large egg, lightly beaten

1. To make the dough, whisk together the flour, sugar, and salt in a large bowl. Mound the mixture, and scoop a well from the center. Add the but-

continued

ter, egg, egg yolks, zest, and rum to the well, and, using your fingers and working outward from the well, mix the dough until it holds together. Pat it into two balls, one slightly larger than the other. Cover them, and set them aside to rest in a cool place or in the refrigerator for at least 1 hour.

2. Preheat the oven to 350°F. Butter a 10-inch pie plate.

3. To prepare the cream, pour all but 2 tablespoons of milk into a saucepan, add the sugar, and bring the mixture to a boil over high heat, stirring to dissolve the sugar. Remove the pan from the heat.

4. In a small bowl, combine the remaining 2 tablespoons milk and the flour, and stir to make a paste. Add this paste and the egg yolks to the milk, and stir. Return the pan to the heat, and cook the mixture over low heat, stirring, for about 5 minutes, until the cream is thickened. Take care that the egg does not scramble. Set the pan aside, and let the cream cool slightly.

5. Add the rum and raisins, if you're using them, and rum to the cooled cream, and stir well.

6. On a lightly floured surface, roll out the larger ball of dough into a circle about 12 inches in diameter. Lay the dough in the tart pan, pressing it over the bottom and about ½ inch up the sides. Pour the cream mixture over the dough.

7. Roll the smaller ball of dough into a circle a little larger than 10 inches in diameter. Lay this over the cream, and gently fold the bottom edge over the top. Brush the top crust with the beaten egg. Bake the tart on the center rack of the oven for about 45 minutes, until the crust is lightly browned. Let the tart cool before serving.

Almond Tart

❖ TARTA DE ALMENDRAS ❖

Serves 8

When I was asked to be the guest chef for a meal honoring Sr. Alvarez del Manzano, the mayor of Madrid, at the Biltmore Hotel in Los Angeles, the menu included this classic Spanish tart. It is so rich and moist, it needs no more garnish than a little *natillas* and a dusting of powdered sugar.

1 cup sugar
1 tablespoon grated lemon zest
½ pound shelled almonds (see Note)
3 large eggs
4 large egg yolks
2 tablespoons unsalted butter, softened
½ cup unbleached all-purpose flour
2 teaspoons baking powder
Pinch of salt
Sweet Basque Cream (page 208)
Confectioners' sugar

1. Preheat the oven to 350°F. Lightly butter a 10-inch pie plate.
2. In a blender, blend the sugar and lemon zest until they are well mixed. Add the almonds, and blend again until the almonds are ground fine. Add the eggs, egg yolks, and butter, and blend until all the contents are well mixed. Transfer the mixture to a bowl.
3. Add the flour, baking powder, and salt, and stir with a spatula or wooden spoon until the dry ingredients are incorporated. Scrape the batter into the pan, and smooth the top. Bake the tart on the center rack of the oven for about 30 minutes, or until a toothpick inserted in the center comes out clean but the tart is still moist. Let it cool on a wire rack.
4. Spoon Sweet Basque Cream onto each plate, and set a tart wedge on top. Sprinkle with confectioners' sugar, and serve.

NOTE: *Almonds, easy to find in any supermarket, are most commonly sold raw or blanched. Buy raw almonds, if possible. Because you will be grinding the nuts, it doesn't matter whether they're whole or sliced when you buy them.*

Grandmother's Creamy Rice

◆ ARROZ CON LECHE DE LA ABUELA ◆

Serves 6 to 8

There are numerous variations of *arroz con leche*, but I particularly like this one. The secret of this creamy dessert is to prepare it as our grandmothers did—with the freshest ingredients and without hurry. With two hours' cooking, the rice can absorb a great deal of milk, becoming very rich and flavorful in the process. For the correct consistency, also, it's important to use medium-grain rather than long-grain rice. This is a good dessert to make when you are tending a more complicated dish for another part of the meal, because the rice requires so little attention.

10 cups whole milk
2 cinnamon sticks
1 strip lemon zest
²/₃ cup raw medium-grain Spanish rice or Italian arborio rice
³/₄ cup sugar
½ cup heavy cream (optional)
Ground cinnamon

1. In a large saucepan, bring the milk to a boil over high heat. Add the cinnamon sticks and lemon zest, and boil for 5 minutes. Reduce the heat to low. Add the rice, and cook, stirring frequently, for about 2 hours, until the mixture is creamy and thick. Take care the rice does not stick (if necessary, use a flame tamer, an iron disk under the pan).

2. Remove the cinnamon sticks and lemon zest, and discard them. Holding the measuring cup high above the pan, pour the sugar through a sieve or sprinkle it over the rice so that the sugar "snows" evenly and lightly over the rice. Continue to cook the rice over very low heat, stirring gently and constantly to prevent burning, for about 15 minutes, until the sugar is incorporated.

3. Remove the pan from the heat and let the rice cool in the pan. If you prefer a very creamy dessert, stir in the cream. Serve the rice in small bowls, sprinkled with cinnamon.

Fried Milk

Serves 4

This truly delicious dessert, sometimes called *leche frita*, in some ways resembles what Americans call French toast. However, similarities end with appearance. The method for making Fried Milk is completely different—for one thing, there is no bread!—and requires far more skill and perseverance. Mostly, you must stand at the stove stirring the milk mixture for at least 20 minutes, until it is creamy and smooth, or the dessert will fail. And then you must be patient and not try to cut the mixture into squares until it is completely cool. If it is even a little warm, it will fall apart when you cut it. *Tostadas de crema* are very good served with caramel sauce.

3 cups whole milk
2 cinnamon sticks
²/₃ cup sugar, plus a little more for sprinkling
¹/₃ cup plus 2 tablespoons unbleached all-purpose flour
¹/₂ cup olive or other vegetable oil (see Note)
2 large eggs, lightly beaten
Ground cinnamon

1. In a saucepan, combine 2 cups of the milk with the cinnamon sticks, and bring the milk to a boil over high heat. Immediately reduce the heat to low. Gradually add the sugar, stirring constantly, until it is dissolved. Remove and discard the cinnamon sticks.

2. In a blender, combine the remaining 1 cup milk and ¹/₃ cup of the flour, and blend until the mixture is smooth. Transfer it to the saucepan, and cook the mixture over medium-low heat, stirring continuously, until it is creamy and smooth. This will take at least 20 minutes. Pour the mixture into a greased jelly-roll pan of about 8 by 10 inches. (The mixture should fill the

continued

pan to a depth of about ½ inch. If it is shallower, use a smaller pan; if it is deeper, use a larger pan.) Let the mixture cool.

3. When the milk mixture is completely cool, cut it into 2-by-2-inch squares.

4. In a large skillet, heat the oil over medium-high heat until it is very hot. Spread the remaining 2 tablespoons flour in a shallow bowl, and put the eggs into another small bowl. Carefully coat both sides of each square with flour, and then dip it in the eggs. Fry the squares in the hot oil, immediately reducing the heat a little as soon as you put the squares into the hot oil. Fry them for 1 minute on each side, and then drain them on paper towels. You will have to do this in batches; reheat the oil between batches.

5. Serve the squares warm or at room temperature, sprinkled with sugar and cinnamon.

NOTE: *I use olive oil at home, but you might prefer a more neutral-tasting oil in this sweet dessert.*

Cream-Cheese Ice Cream with Red Berry Sauce

❖ HELADO DE QUESO FRESCO CON SALSA DE FRUTOS ROJOS ❖

Serves 6

Unlike all the other desserts in this chapter, this one isn't a Basque classic, but I decided to include it anyway because it's so good and so popular today with the people of San Sebastián (Donostia). The dessert was developed by Juan Mari Arzak, the chief-proprietor of San Sebastián's three-star Michelin restaurant, Arzak. Chef Arzak makes the ice cream with fresh cow's milk cheese that he buys from local cheesemakers, but I have substituted ordinary cream cheese (I use the Philadelphia brand), and found that the ice cream still tastes great. It looks very pretty when matched with the deep red sauce.

1 pound cream cheese (two 8-ounce packages)
1 cup whole milk
1 cup heavy cream
²/₃ cup sugar

1 cup water
3 tablespoons sugar
1 pound berries, such as raspberries, strawberries, red currants, or a combination

. . .

2 to 3 tablespoons heavy cream

1. To make the ice cream, combine the cream cheese, milk, cream, and sugar in a food processor or blender, and blend until the mixture is smooth (if you're using a blender, do this in batches). Strain the mixture into the container of an ice-cream maker, and freeze according to the manufacturer's instructions. This ice cream will freeze in less time than others.

2. To make the sauce, combine the water and sugar in a small saucepan, and cook over medium-high heat until the sugar dissolves.

3. Transfer the syrup to a blender, add the berries, and purée them. Strain the sauce into a glass or ceramic container to rid it of seeds. Cover the container, and refrigerate it for at least 2 hours, until the sauce is well chilled.

4. Spoon the sauce into shallow soup bowls. Using two soup spoons, form the ice cream into quenelle shapes, and place three on top of the sauce in each bowl. Garnish each dish by dribbling a little heavy cream over the sauce.

NOTE: *If you do not have an ice-cream maker, transfer the strained ice cream mixture to a shallow metal bowl. Freeze the mixture for 8 hours, stirring it every 30 minutes with a spatula to aerate it and insure a creamy consistency.*

Chestnut Soup

Serves 6

€uropeans have always loved chestnuts, and nowhere is this appreciation more evident than in this sweet dessert soup. According to all accounts, the soup has been made since very early times in the rural areas of Navarra, adjacent to the Basque Country. Interestingly, across the border in the French Basque country, you will find a similar soup made with the addition of vegetables and served as an appetizer.

Because this soup is so rich and because chestnuts are in season in the fall, I usually serve it on chilly nights. I like to cook it in a glazed earthenware casserole, in the tradition of the Basque Country.

½ pound chestnuts, in the shell
2½ cups whole milk
1 cinnamon stick
2 tablespoons sugar, plus a little more for sprinkling
3 to 4 slices white bread
Ground cinnamon

1. Preheat the oven to 400°F.
2. Using a sharp knife, slit the flat side of each chestnut, and lay the chestnuts in a single layer on an ungreased baking sheet. Roast them for about 15 minutes, until they are fragrant. Remove the baking sheet from the oven, but do not turn the oven off. When the chestnuts are cool enough to handle, shell them, and transfer the nutmeats to a saucepan.
3. Add the milk to the pan, and heat it over medium-high heat until it boils. Add the cinnamon stick and 2 tablespoons sugar, reduce the heat to low, and simmer gently for about 15 minutes, stirring several times, until the nuts are soft.
4. Strain the milk into a casserole or clay dish, reserving the nutmeats. Lay the bread slices on top of the milk, and sprinkle them with sugar and cin-

namon. Put the dish into the oven for about 10 minutes, until the bread and milk crust over. (Alternatively, you can set the dish under the broiler for several minutes, until the bread and milk crust over. If you use a broiler, though, watch carefully to prevent scorching.) Garnish with the chestnuts, and serve.

Creamy Walnut Purée

♦ INTXAURSALSA CON HELADO DE VAINILLA ♦

Serves 4

My good friend Felisa Madariaga, who owns one of the loveliest Basque farmhouses I have ever seen, always treats me to special Basque dishes whenever I visit to buy choricero peppers, which she dries in glorious bunches hanging from the front of the house. This luscious dessert is one of her specialties, and well worth the time it takes to make it. Use high-quality vanilla ice cream, or treat yourself to scoops of the Cream-Cheese Ice Cream on page 214. It is interesting to note that whereas the Romans introduced "English" walnuts to Europe, it was Basque sailors who carried them to California, which today is a major producer of the nuts. Be sure to cook the purée for at least 30 minutes, longer if you prefer it thicker.

1/2 pound shelled walnuts
4 cups water
1 cinnamon stick
4 cups whole milk
1 cup sugar
Vanilla ice cream

continued

1. Using a mortar and pestle, crush the walnuts until they are ground fine but not quite a paste. (You can use a food processor for this if you take great care not to overprocess the nuts.)

2. In a large saucepan, combine the water and cinnamon stick. Bring the water to a boil over high heat. Add the walnuts, reduce the heat to medium, and cook for about 20 minutes, until the water is almost completely evaporated and the ground nuts are very thick. Discard the cinnamon stick.

3. Add the milk and sugar to the saucepan, and cook over medium-low heat, stirring occasionally, for about 30 minutes, until the mixture is slightly thickened. If you'd like a thicker mixture, cook it for 5 to 10 minutes more, or even longer. Let the purée cool in the pan, and then cover and chill the purée for at least 2 hours.

4. Spoon the purée into small bowls, and top each serving with a scoop of ice cream. Serve immediately.

PACHARÁN

❧ *Although it is made* in Navarra, *pacharán* is a popular liqueur throughout the Basque Country. We serve it poured over ice as a sweet after-dinner drink. Pacharán is made by adding sloeberries (*endrinas*) and three or four coffee beans to a bottle of *anis* (anisette). The mixture is allowed to age in a dark place for several months. The result is a golden-red liqueur. Pacharán is available in liquor stores in the United States.

Pears with Red Rioja Wine

❖ PERAS AL VINO TINTO DE RIOJA ❖

Serves 4

When the weather is warm, serve the pears and sauce cold or at room temperature. When the weather is cold, serve both pears and sauce warm. For a decorative touch, make several parallel incisions along each pear half, leaving the base intact, and then fan the pieces. Garnish with mint leaves placed under the stem end of each pear.

4 large, firm pears, such as Bosc or Bartlett, peeled, halved lengthwise, and cored
4 cups red Rioja wine
²/₃ cup sugar
1 cinnamon stick
2 tablespoons strawberry or raspberry preserves

1. In a saucepan just large enough to hold them comfortably, combine the pears with the wine, sugar, and cinnamon stick. Bring the contents to a boil over high heat. Reduce the heat to low, and cook for about 30 minutes, until the pears are fork-tender. Lift the pears from the pan, and set them aside to cool.
2. Remove and discard the cinnamon stick. Add the preserves to the pan, raise the heat, and boil for about 5 minutes, stirring constantly, until the preserves melt and the sauce is smooth.
3. Serve two pear halves on each plate, and spoon the sauce over them.

Apple Tart

◆ TARTA DE MANZANA MODERNA ◆

Serves 8

Any student of French cuisine will recognize the similarity between this tart and *tarte tatin*, the upside-down apple tart so beloved for its lightly caramelized apples. The Basque version is equally tempting and delicious, and, because my recipe calls for store-bought puff pastry, the preparation is very simple. I like to serve this with Sweet Basque Cream (page 208).

1 teaspoon unsalted butter
1 cup sugar
8 tart green apples, such as Granny Smith or Fuji, peeled, cored,
and cut into 6 wedges each
2 sheets commercial puff pastry (see Note)

1. Preheat the oven to 300°F.
2. Spread the butter on the bottom and sides of a 10-inch pie plate.
3. In a very heavy saucepan (preferably copper), cook the sugar over low heat, stirring occasionally with a wooden spoon, for 5 to 6 minutes, until the sugar melts. Raise the heat slightly, and cook for about 5 minutes longer, washing the sugar crystals down the side of the pan with a pastry brush dipped in a cup of ice water. As soon as the sugar turns a caramel color, pour it into the pie plate, tipping the plate so the sugar covers the bottom and flows up the side. Take care when handling the caramelized sugar; it is very hot.
4. Lay the apple wedges over the sugar, arranging them so that the broad sides lie flat on the bottom in concentric circles. Fill in the gaps with the remaining wedges, narrow sides down, broad sides up.
5. Lay the sheets of puff pastry over the apples, overlapping the sheets. Tuck in the puff pastry at the edge of the pie plate, and trim off the excess.

6. Bake the tart on the center rack of the oven for about 1 hour, until the crust is golden brown. Set the tart in its pan on a wire rack, and let it rest until the crust is cool; the apples should still be warm. Invert the tart onto a platter, cut it into wedges, and serve it warm.

NOTE: *Although you can use homemade puff pastry for this tart, the commercial brands available in the freezer sections of many supermarkets are very good and save time and effort.*

Christmas Fruit Compote

◆ COMPOTA DE NAVIDAD ◆

Serves 10

After a sumptuous Christmas Eve meal, it is traditional to serve this sweet yet light compote. Although it can be eaten warm, I prefer it cold. The combination of fruits here is typical, but you can vary them to suit your own tastes.

2 pounds tart apples, such as Granny Smith or Fuji, peeled, cored,
and cut into small wedges
2 pounds pears, peeled, cored, and cut into small wedges
1 quart water
1½ cups sugar
1 cinnamon stick
Juice of ½ lemon
½ cup prunes
⅓ cup raisins
⅓ cup dried apricots
1½ cups red Rioja wine

continued

1. In a stockpot, combine the apples, pears, and water, and bring the contents to a boil over high heat. Reduce the heat, and add the sugar, cinnamon stick, and lemon juice. Simmer the mixture over medium heat for about 15 minutes, stirring to prevent scorching.

2. While the mixture simmers, combine the prunes, raisins, and apricots with the wine in a saucepan, and bring the contents to a boil over high heat. Reduce the heat, and simmer over medium heat for about 10 minutes, until the fruits plump and soften.

3. Add the prunes, raisins, and apricots and any remaining wine to the pot containing the apples and pears. Stir to mix the fruits, and simmer them for about 10 minutes, until the flavors blend and the apples and pears are soft. Serve the compote warm, or refrigerate it in a covered container, and serve it later chilled.

TWELFTH NIGHT IN THE BASQUE COUNTRY

❧ *For many children* in the Western world, Christmas Eve, December 24, is the most exciting night of the year. For Basque children the most exciting night is January 5, when they prepare for the next day's Twelfth Night celebration. On the fifth, children throughout the Basque Country eagerly polish their shoes, and then each family displays the clean, neat shoes in a circle in the center of the living room. Alongside the shoes, they leave a tray of sweets, three glasses of brandy, and a jug of water. Just as children elsewhere wait for Santa Claus on December 24, Basque children wait for the Three Wise Men to bring them gifts on January 5. The sweets and brandy are for Melchor, Gaspar, and Baltasar, the Wise Men, and the water is for their camels. When the children wake on January 6, they find their shoes filled with gifts and sweet treats—unless they have been very naughty, in which case the shoes are supposed to be stuffed with charcoal. I don't think much charcoal is ever in evidence, though, on that joyous morning.

Figs with Natillas

Serves 4

People have always appreciated the fig, a tree as primordial as it looks; archeologists have discovered traces of the tree's leaves and fruit among European prehistoric remains. Once you taste a fig, you understand why the small, not-too-sweet fruit has been so cherished that today a basket of figs still symbolizes friendship, prosperity, and good luck. (The notable exception to this is the basket of figs given Cleopatra; a deadly asp was coiled beneath the fruit!) Although to my knowledge there is only one word for "fig" in English, in Spanish we have two words. *Brebas* refers to purple figs, and *higos* to green ones. Both have very short seasons—*brebas* in July and *higos* in August—which explains the Spanish expression "*de higos a brebas*," which roughly translates as "August till July" and means the same as the expression "once in a blue moon." For a brief time in midsummer, however, the seasons overlap, and you can get both kinds of figs. I always take advantage of this short interlude to serve two together in this simple way.

12 green figs, trimmed (not peeled)
12 purple figs, trimmed (not peeled)
1 cup Sweet Basque Cream (page 208)
¼ cup chopped walnuts

1. Cut the figs approximately in half crosswise.
2. Spoon the Sweet Basque Cream over the bottom of each plate. Arrange three purple fig halves and three green fig halves on each plate, cut sides up, in a circle of alternating colors. Sprinkle them with the chopped walnuts, and serve.

Quince Jam

Serves 4

Y̲ou may be surprised by this dessert. It's a sweet concentration of cooked quince and sugar that is allowed to harden and then is served with fresh cheese or a semicured Manchego for a delightful and very unusual ending to a meal. I learned how to make this from my friend Juanjo Urtasum, a Navarran diplomat currently posted in Brazil. Because he shares my passion for food, we frequently trade recipes, regardless of where we are living. This one is from his 85-year-old aunt, who still makes the dessert, and it has become one of my very favorites.

For this recipe you will need a scale, since both the quince and sugar must be weighed.

4 quinces
Sugar

1. Wash the quinces, but do not peel them. Put them into a large saucepan, and add enough water to cover them by 1 inch. Bring the water to a boil over high heat. Reduce the heat to medium, and cook the quinces for about 40 minutes, until they begin to crack. With a slotted spoon, remove the quinces from the pan, and set them aside to cool.

2. When the quinces are cool enough to handle, peel them, and remove and discard the seeds. Weigh the peeled and seeded quinces, and then pass them through a food mill.

3. Transfer the quinces to a saucepan, and add the same weight of sugar as fruit. Stir well, and cook the mixture over very low heat for about 1 hour, stirring constantly with a wooden spoon, until the mixture turns red and very sticky.

4. Spoon the jam into a clean cloth napkin, and squeeze out any remaining liquid. Transfer the jam to shallow containers, and let it cool uncovered. Cut it when it has solidified. It will keep in the refrigerator, tightly covered, for up to 2 months.

Index